T0193215

THE
ROAD OF

THIRTY DAYS OF DELIVERANCE

ELIÉZER MAGALHÃES

WESTBOW
PRESS®
A DIVISION OF THOMAS NELSON
& ZONDERVAN

WestBow Press books may be ordered through booksellers or by contacting:

WestBow Press
A Division of Thomas Nelson & Zondervan
1663 Liberty Drive
Bloomington, IN 47403
www.westbowpress.com
844-714-3454

Holy Bible, New International Version®, NIV® Copyright ©1973, 1978, 1984, 2011 by Biblica, Inc.® Used by permission. All rights reserved worldwide.

ISBN: 978-1-6642-9645-9 (sc)
ISBN: 978-1-6642-9643-5 (hc)
ISBN: 978-1-6642-9644-2 (e)

Library of Congress Control Number: 2023905892

Print information available on the last page.

WestBow Press rev. date: 04/03/2023

Contents

Introduction

The great adventure of life was planned by God. We are his creatures, made to be his sons and daughters. However, our story took a turn when we turned away from God. Since then, we have wandered along the roads of life. Some followed the path of pleasure, others the path of money, and still others the path of fame. A sick and turbulent society has sprung up everywhere. The father of all this confusion was Satan, the same serpent that one day deceived Adam and Eve. He invented false gods, raised false prophets, and began to lead people in dangerous ways.

Even though we left the house of God, we forgot the way back. Even if we wanted to, we would be unable to return alone as humanity is now controlled by occult forces that enslave it. However, the Heavenly Father did not abandon us, sending his Son to show us the way back home! Jesus came down to our world so you could go up with him to heaven. The road he presents to us is long and narrow, but he assures us that he will be with us for the whole walk!

In this book, I present to you *The Road of Freedom*. This is not any road, because every other road will take you back to suffering and slavery. You can't ask someone to walk in your place. This is not a walk through your strength but through faith in God's strength.

I recommend that you read a chapter per day. Do not merely read it, but meditate on every verse quoted. Pray in each assignment proposed. It is good if you do the assignments with a brother or sister in Christ helping you! Allow God to speak to your heart.

Now put on your hiking shoes and hit this road!

Day 1

CREATED TO BE HIS CHILDREN

If you were transported to the time of creation, with the privilege of watching God shaping the universe, you would be amazed to see the appearance of light through a simple word spoken by him. In amazement, you would observe the separation between the dry ground and the waters on the surface of the globe, watching the Creator carving the outline of a living sculpture with his own hands. You would witness the thriving of plants in various forms, colors, and smells, sublimely disclosing the living canvas painted by the Creator.

You would also see the Lord creating animals in their uncountable types and sizes, placing them on the surface of the earth, in the waters, and in the heavens. And finally, you would witness God designing his masterpiece—the human being. You would see the Eternal molding the first humans with his own hands, delineating man and woman as his own image and likeness. And you would lose your breath as you watched the Creator of the universe himself blowing into the nostrils of an earth doll, turning the inanimate into a living being.

When we talk about the wonders of creation, we cannot help but mention that, before we knew the truth described in scripture, you and I were born in a home that did not know the whole revealed truth of God. For before the new birth, described by Jesus in John 3:5–7, we all had wrong concepts regarding our origin. Consequently, we need to be clear about the biblical truth that the world and everything in it was made by the One God. The same who came down from heaven and incarnated as Jesus Christ, disclosing himself to us!

When talking about the creation, I cannot help but compare it to what happens when a couple is waiting for the delivery of a son or daughter. Usually, a place is separated in the house, which is arranged and decorated in the most delightful and charming way. Some furniture is bought, with the baby crib as the coziest item in the bedroom. Toys, clothes, and other objects are placed with great care.

Everything is done with love and perfection for the loved one who will arrive. And finally, when the nine months of pregnancy are over, that little human—the image and likeness of his or her parents—is finally born. Now the baby can enjoy the parents' affection, love, and relationship in this beautiful place that was prepared specifically for him or her.

This is the picture portrayed in the world's creation: A God who prepares everything for the arrival of his son and daughter. The Creator organized the world for the advent of the ones who would be his image, the object of his love. They would call him Father, and he would call them his children. You and I were created to be sons and daughters of God, to have a divine and eternal fellowship with the Creator.

When the Lord created the human being, he himself said that this was "very good," meaning pleasant, satisfying. Our creation brought happiness to God's heart; maybe it was the same kind that a father and mother have when giving birth to a son or daughter. Unlike the rest of the creation, which God declared "was good," man and woman were declared "very good," indicating how delighted the Creator was!

And we read in the book of Genesis that the Lord spoke face-to-face with Adam and Eve. The Creator walked with them in the Garden of Eden. We could express the same astonishment as the psalmist did, uttering Psalm 8:3–4, "When I consider your heavens, the work of your fingers, the moon and the stars which you have set in place, what is man that you are mindful of him, the son of man that you care for him?" Why would the Almighty God walk with his creation if not because they were made to be his children?

What a great experience it would be to enjoy moments like those that Adam and Eve had with the Creator. We can only imagine the type of relationship they had when there was yet no evil. Man and woman were still not separated from God!

It reminds me when my first daughter was born and I experienced the joy of taking her home from the maternity hospital. The satisfaction was too great to fit inside me. And I believe this feeling is a small reflection of God's enigmatic love for us. He imprinted deep inside man and woman a love and other inexplicable feelings for their children that points, even though superficially, to his deeper love and care for us.

Nevertheless, we know that our history had a sad twist causing the calamitous and suffering condition in which humanity is found today. I know that not all fathers and mothers love their children as they were supposed to, for there is something wrong in the creation today, within every one of us! An angelic invader infiltrated the Garden of Eden and, according to Genesis 3, implanted a seed of imperfection in a perfect world. This seed is called sin, and we will talk more about it in the next chapter. But for now, we must look at God's original creation, his love, his original plan, and the fact that you were created to be his image and likeness.

The original creation was made without sin, evil, or sickness and without negligent or evil parents, violence, corruption, or any type of deceit. This was the purpose for humanity from our Creator, the Eternal Father. Because humanity lost the meaning of their lives over the years, suffering and sin have overshadowed who God really is, and who we are for him. Sin blurs our perception of God, ourselves, and others.

Like seeing through a cracked lens, our spiritual eyes are unable to see the world in any other fashion than through our sin. Only a purified gaze allows us to properly appreciate the loving God who continues to look for a relationship with lost sons and daughters. Only when we understand this love can we grasp why the Creator became a baby, Jesus Christ, who grew up and offered himself in sacrifice "as a ransom for many" (Matthew 20:28).

Scripture reveals that God wants to have a relationship with us, without the impediments of sin. This is for God's enjoyment and also ours because there is no enjoyment outside God's delight. And the Bible shows how the Creator planned to bring back those who were lost to him! As we walk through the pages of scripture, we observe the Almighty Father building the way back to his home for us. It is a path that crosses the valley of renunciation and traverses the bridge of the cross in faith.

It is the path of deliverance from sin, the devil, and the powers of a fallen flesh! This path has a name, Jesus Christ, and it is walked by repentance faith! My questions now are these: Are you walking on this path, or do you just know it from hearing about it? Have you crossed the bridge, or do you just see it from afar? How about, starting today, you put your feet on the road of the most important journey of your life?

Come with us on this way back to the Father's house, for he is waiting for you!

> Make the following prayer:

Lord and God, Creator of all heavens and earth, I invite you to speak to me during these days that I will be doing this devotional. Please help me to return to the place where you live. Show me the way, because I am lost. I want to hear your voice and be able to call you Father. I am a sinner and confess that I need your salvation! I believe Jesus is the way, and even though I don't understand everything, I want to trust him with all my heart. All I want is to be your son/daughter and rest peacefully in your presence forever. In Jesus's name, amen!

Day 2

THE ORIGIN OF EVIL

I was seventeen years old when I realized there was something wrong with me. I was walking in the back of the house, going toward my bedroom, which was at the end of the backyard at the time, when my dog came running, all happy to welcome me. For more than twelve years, my dog played with me. But that day, when he climbed up on me all joyful while I was walking, I kicked him so hard that he was thrown a meter away, unleashing a yelp of pain.

I was very angry, for some reason that I don't remember, and I took my anger out on the poor animal. In fact, *I* was the animal in that moment! That dog was already old and, crying quietly, went back to his house. It was after the anger passed that I realized what I had done. For some days, my dog avoided me, visibly afraid of other aggressions.

Have you ever looked in the mirror without recognizing yourself? Have you ever found feelings and desires that seem to be alien, which many times dominated you? Something that is not you but is inward? Did you ever have to deal with guilt or shame after doing what you promised yourself you would never do again? If we are entirely honest, we need to acknowledge that there is something wrong with us. The apostle Paul expressed this same perception when he wrote,

> For I know that good itself does not dwell in me,
> that is, in my sinful nature. For I have the desire to
> do what is good, but I cannot carry it out. For I do

5

not do the good I want to do, but the evil I do not want to do—this I keep on doing. (Romans 7:18–19)

Some people learn as children that the origin of human problems comes from the law of karma—from the experiences people had in past lives. However, the scriptures show that the belief in reincarnation is a lie! For the Bible declares that "people are destined to die once, and after that to face judgment" (Hebrews 9:27). Other people think that evil is part of destiny, thinking that God is the author of evil and is responsible for choosing those who will be good and those who are not. These people believe that everything happening, good or evil, is determined by God. But scripture shows that evil was the result of our chosen disobedience, where everything started in the Garden of Eden.

The Creator placed a tree in the middle of the Garden in order to test the faithfulness of Adam and Eve. God's order was that they should not eat the fruit of this tree (Genesis 2:17), and the penalty for disobedience was death. To obey meant to submit to the Father, but to disobey would be to submit to death. You may think that the penalty was too terrible, which indeed it was, but if we remember that life itself flows from God, we will understand that to be separated from him is indeed to die. Death is separation from God; therefore, living separated from the Creator is to live death itself. But living in relationship with God is to live grounded in the source of life.

The book of Genesis explains that a serpent approached Eve asking if God had forbidden eating from all the trees of the Garden. Eve readily explained that they could eat from all, for the prohibition was regarding the one in the middle of the Garden. The serpent's words had poison as it implied that God was evil, forbidding humankind to eat any fruit. Behind the question was the idea that God was not telling everything and he was not good. The serpent's plan was to sow a seed of doubt and frustration in Eve's heart. By taking her attention away from all that was given so graciously by God, turning her focus on the only fruit she could not possess, the serpent started the temptation.

Every time we move our eyes away from what God gave us and put them on things that he did not give, we are tempted to be frustrated. We can start thinking, as Eve did, that we deserve what was forbidden because maybe God does not know what is best for us! By doing that, we neglect the whole Garden given by God, exchanging his eternal delights for temporal things.

The serpent questioned Eve's certainties, trying to convince her that by eating the fruit she would become like God. The Bible reveals that behind that serpent was a very astute spiritual being (Revelation 20:2). It was an angel created by God who had rebelled, however, and aspired to drag humanity with it. Scripture calls this fallen angel Satan, which simply means "the enemy." The Bible does not explain all the details about how Satan fell but gives some information. We know, for example, that he dragged a third of the angels of God with him (Revelation 12:4), and the scripture calls them demons. They cooperate with Satan, opposing God and seeking to destroy humanity.

Although Satan was guilty of lying, manipulating Adam and Eve into disobedience, it was the man and the woman who made the decision to believe in God or in the serpent. Eve chose to eat the fruit and so did Adam, because he was with her. Maybe he had heard the whole conversation and didn't say anything. Perhaps Adam shared her decision, or maybe he silenced himself neglecting his responsibility to prevent Eve's sin. What we do know for sure is that the consequence of disobedience affected them both, for God held man and woman equally responsible for deliberately choosing to disobey him.

Some may say it is strange to think that a simple act of eating a fruit could cause all the evils in the world, but it is important to understand that what was at stake was the faithfulness of the human being. I met a pastor of a church who on one occasion succumbed to the charms of a beautiful young lady who was not his wife, giving her a kiss in a moment of weakness. Nothing else happened after that kiss, but his marriage was never the same. In a short time, he got divorced and lost his ministry. His wife and church never trusted him again. What power lies in a simple and apparently naïve act!

When I was a teenager, I worked fixing electronic devices in a maintenance shop. One of the men who worked with me one day decided to steal some money from our boss: $3. The money was in a drawer, and he thought our boss would not perceive the theft of a small amount of money. He was discovered and immediately fired. I remember the shame on his face when he left the place. What are $3 worth in terms of honor and dignity? Why dismiss someone for so little? We know that someone who steals $3 today can one day steal a thousand or more. After all, as usually said, character is what we do when no one is watching! Adam and Eve's loyalty were at stake, and they failed. What about you? How many times did you fail when no one was watching?

When Adam and Eve ate that fruit, they made a faith decision: to believe in God, who warned about the danger of death, or believe in the serpent. The flavor of the forbidden fruit was not as sweet as they expected, and the status they reached was not what they imagined. With the decision they made, the relationship with the Father was broken, as with each other and inwardly with themselves.

Disobeying God represented submitting to Satan, for they disbelieved God's Word, desiring to be like God. Consequently, death came to have power over both, as well as over all things that were under human authority. We know that the kingdom of death belongs to Satan (Hebrews 2:14), and through sin, humankind was placed under his authority. Satan is called the prince of this world (John 12:31 and 16:11), prince of the power of the air (Ephesians 2:2), and god of this age (2 Corinthians 4:4). That is the reason why today we live in a world where death, diseases, mental pathologies, social disturbances, divorce, murders, addictions, wars, corruption, pandemics, and even natural catastrophes are everywhere, all of which are directly related to human sinfulness. The apostle Paul wrote that nature "was subjected to futility, not by its own choice, but because of the will of him who subjected it," and that it is "groaning as in the pains of childbirth" (Romans 8:20–22). The whole world is suffering because of our sins.

The origin of all evil experienced comes from this historical and unique fact, but also from our own personal sins that we daily commit in servitude to the prince of this world. As Adam and Eve did, every one of us follows the same evil example when we sin.

The offenders disobey God, bringing shame to his name, and they are clearly two: Satan and the human being. It is important to emphasize that even when someone suffers immense pressure from the tempter, he is still responsible for his own decisions and, therefore, consequences. In the end, it is you who says yes or no to the seductions of the forbidden fruits of this world! Satan is to blame, but we should not neglect our responsibility! You and I are not innocent! We are all under the shame of sinfulness in front of the holy God. We deserve death as punishment because we all broke God's law!

That's why our journey must start from the simple truth that we are guilty, under shame, and therefore condemned! Sin is like a spiritual virus that infected us because it was transmitted to all humanity. It is the most damaging pandemic in human history because it not only kills physically but spiritually and eternally!

You, I, and billions of people were infected by this disease a long time ago. Your brain, body, thoughts, desires, and emotions are under its influence. It makes you hurt the people you should love, speak what you shouldn't, and do what you don't want to do. You often find yourself controlled by imprisoning feelings because of it. It is not you, but at the same time, it is! Sin has turned brothers against brothers, husbands against wives, and nations against nations because in essence sin is humanity against God!

However, do not despair, for there is a vaccine, although many still do not know. The only vaccine for this spiritual virus is Jesus Christ, who came to this world and never sinned. Jesus is God himself descending as a human being to heal us from the wound caused by the serpent. Jesus's death on the cross was the payment for our sins, where he removed our shame assuming it for himself. Jesus died in our shame so we could live according to his honor. He substituted us in our condemnation, dying as a ransom for us!

As Jesus said, "For God so loved the world that he gave his one and only Son, that whoever believes in him shall not perish but have eternal life" (John 3:16). The cure is to believe wholeheartedly in

Jesus Christ and follow him, because he is the only "way" (John 14:6), the road we all must take to return to God's home!

In Jesus our sins are inoculated, and we are freed from Satan's power. Jesus pays our debt freely, restores our relationship with the Father, washing us of all shame, because he redirected all the wrath upon himself. Through Jesus's sacrifice, he cut the ties that Satan and his demons had over our lives. Nevertheless, if you have difficulties accepting this cure, do not be deceived; it is the virus interfering with your reasoning. It is still in control. Trust in Jesus and see! Pray for his deliverance within you and you will see his power.

After sinning, Adam and Eve were expelled from the Garden of Eden. In fact, they expelled themselves as they knew the repercussions of disobeying God's command. They abandoned the house of God just like the prodigal son in the parable told by Jesus (Luke 15:11–32). We turned our backs on the Father and decided to live independently of him.

Are you trying to live independently of God? Can you perceive sin in your own life? Can you notice attitudes, choices, or words you have said that you should never have said or things you should never have done? Do you have a deep sense of guilt or shame, thinking that if possible, you would go back in time to change what you did? Are you dominated by fear in facing the consequences of your sins? Are you overwhelmed by anger because of your sins and the sins of others, with the desire to burn the world because of its injustice? To be truly free of these things and become God's children, we need to solve the problem of sin, which only happens by believing, trusting in Jesus, and surrendering our lives entirely into his hands! Jesus came to give us abundant life (John 10:10)! Do you want it?

Make this prayer:

Dear Lord Jesus, I confess that I am a sinner. I admit that I have sinned and failed to obey your will. Open my eyes, enabling me to see the sin within me in such a way that I repent completely, abandoning everything that has alienated me from You! I believe in Jesus Christ, and I trust in your salvation. I accept your sacrifice on the cross in my place. I give you my life entirely! I ask you to forgive all of my sins, wash me from my shame, quench my wrath, and restore my relationship with the Father. Please come within my heart and change me, because I desperately need to be born again, to be born from above. Thank you, Jesus, because I know you are answering my prayer, and now I am a new creature! Today I begin a journey with you. Thank you, Jesus!

Day 3

THE GREAT DECEPTION

After the fall of Adam and Eve and their separation from God, an existential emptiness began to take over the hearts of humanity. An inward longing for God took over their hearts in such a way that they sought to quench their thirst by manufacturing imaginary substitutes. Satan began to explore this inner vulnerability, leading people to fashion gods for themselves that could momentarily fill this emptiness. Sometimes Satan himself presented in different forms to deceive men, to lead them astray! The substitution of God is called idolatry!

Human beings began to imagine for themselves particular gods with the intention of supplying the desires of their own corrupted hearts. Ancient civilizations began to believe in false gods. There were gods of rain, sun, war, love, sex, wealth, and several others who dominated various spheres of life. These gods received their own names, and in the Bible, they appear many times, such as Baal, Moloch, and Astaroth. Men worshiped nature, the wind, the sun, the lakes, and the trees, confusing creation with the Creator. This mentality was found among the ancient Egyptians, Sumerians, Babylonians, Greeks, Nordics, Indians, and many others.

This same mentality can still be found in many current religions that believe in different spiritual entities for each area of life. Sometimes, for example, they are called spirits of nature in animist religions, gods for the Hindus, genies (or djinn) for Muslims, or bodhisattvas for Buddhists. For them, human needs can be answered by a spiritual entity to be sought, revered, and consulted. Some even conceive the idea of a supreme God, creator of all things, but for them, he is very distant and inaccessible. Even the Muslims, who claim to believe in one God, in fact treat him as very distant and inaccessible, falling into different types of idolatry. The Bible calls this idolatry, which is nothing more than to worship a false god or idol who can be a person, alive or dead, a false prophet, or a spiritual being, a demon, or an angel, or even an object, like an amulet, an image, a sculpture, that replaces the true God. If you put your faith in anything different from God, it is idolatry! Satan takes advantage of these idols invented by the human mind, sometimes even giving "life" to some, attracting worship to himself by deceiving the nations.

When God gave the Ten Commandments to Moses, in Exodus 20, he made it clear in the first six verses that he required exclusivity in worship for he would not tolerate any kind of idolatry. Read below the order given by God.

> And God spoke all these words: I am the LORD your God, who brought you out of Egypt, out of the land of slavery. You shall have no other gods before me. You shall not make for yourself an image in the form of anything in heaven above or on the earth beneath or in the waters below. You shall not bow down to them or worship them; for I, the LORD your God, am a jealous God, punishing the children for the sin of the parents to the third and fourth generation of those who hate me, but showing love to a thousand generations of those who love me and keep my commandments. (Exodus 20:1–6)

God commanded that no image or sculpture should be made in order to be worshiped, whether representing something or someone from heaven, earth, or water. Even an image that could represent God himself was forbidden. The Bible is full of expressions that condemn idolatry. See below some biblical texts that explicitly speak about this.

> All who make idols are nothing, and the things they treasure are worthless. Those who would speak up for them are blind; they are ignorant, to their own shame. Who shapes a god and casts an idol, which can profit nothing? People who do that will be put to shame; such craftsmen are only human beings. Let them all come together and take their stand; they will be brought down to terror and shame. (Isaiah 44:9–11)

> From the rest he makes a god, his idol; he bows down to it and worships. He prays to it and says, "Save me! You are my god." They know nothing, they understand nothing; their eyes are plastered over so they cannot see, and their minds closed so they cannot understand. (Isaiah 44:17–18)

> Gather together and come; assemble, you fugitives from the nations. Ignorant are those who carry about idols of wood, who pray to gods that cannot save. (Isaiah 45:20)

> Do I mean then that a sacrifice offered to an idol is anything, or that an idol is anything? No, but the sacrifices of pagans are offered to demons, not to God, and I do not want you to be participants with demons. You cannot drink the cup of the Lord and the cup of demons too; you cannot have a part in both the Lord's table and the table of demons. (1 Corinthians 10:19–21)

This last text in particular is very important because the apostle Paul explains that behind an idol is a demon at work. Whether a person makes a sacrifice, a prayer, a service, a worship, or reverence that is not directed to the one God, it is directed to demons. To serve idols is to serve Satan! Whether the image is of Baal, Shiva, Buddha, a bodhisattva, the spirits in the woods, or any creature of other human mythology, they are all used by Satan to deceive people! Every idol is a deception that replaces the true God connecting the worshiper to Satan.

Of all the sins against God, idolatry seems to be the sin most commonly found throughout the Bible. Idolatry is frequently compared to the sin of adultery or prostitution (Ezekiel 16:23; Hosea 1:2, 3:1; Jeremiah 3:6–11; James 4:4–5). This is because exchanging God for some other being, whatever it may be, is a betrayal equal to adultery. God feels betrayed, deeply offended, and rejected. Imagine if your spouse from time to time looked for another person to have a loving relationship with. What if your spouse had a secret relationship with someone? See what James says.

> You adulterous people, don't you know that friendship with the world means enmity against God? Therefore, anyone who chooses to be a friend of the world becomes an enemy of God. Or do you think Scripture says without reason that he jealously longs for the spirit he has caused to dwell in us? (James 4:4–5)

God is jealous of you. He doesn't want you to have any other god, idol, person, or object that takes his place in your life. If God is not unique and enough for you, it is not possible to have a relationship with him. He does not want to "date" you or have an "affair." He is not a genie of a magical lamp that we can access and ask whatever we want. He wants relationship and commitment! That is why the Bible calls Jesus "the bridegroom" and the church "the bride" (Luke 5:34; Revelation 19:7).

At this point, I want to ask you this: do you have idols in your heart? Maybe they are visible and you have put them somewhere in your house. Or maybe they are invisible, like something in your heart that substitutes God for you. A good way to identify this type of idol is by asking ourselves these questions: What fills my agenda? What is the force that moves me every day to do what I do? What dominates my thoughts? What is my greatest desire? What is my greatest fear? Am I serving this desire or fear, whereby my life is spinning around it?

What about deciding to give your life only to God? What about rejecting all false gods, idols, in your heart for a full commitment with the Creator? To do this, you need to totally trust in Jesus, resting in him, believing that he will take care of you.

When we decide that the Lord is our only God, we need to renounce our idols, gods, and spirits. God knows our heart. He knows who you have served until today. We must break with each idol, spiritual entity, false god, or any substitute of God in our hearts, affirming in prayer that now our life belongs to Jesus Christ alone, renouncing by name to every alliance made previously with each false god.

Pray like this:

Dear Lord, help me to see what has taken your place in my heart. Help me to identify the idols, the false gods, and to break up any relationship I have with each one of them. What I want is to be exclusive to you, Lord! Forgive me for hurting your heart, offending you by betraying with other gods. Create in me, oh Father, a heart totally turned to you so that I renounce the relationships I have with these idols. In the name of Jesus Christ, I pray to you. Amen.

Now for each idol you have identified, pray this:

I renounce the false god of _____, rejecting him with all my heart to be out of my life. In Jesus's name, get out, _____. Thank you, Jesus, because my life belongs to you!

Day 4

IDOLATRY AND THE CHURCH

U nfortunately, many sincere people have been deceived by Satan and his demons, even within the church. Remember that idolatry is any form of worship, prayer, and reverence for something or someone other than the Creator himself. The idolatry within the church arose at the beginning of the Middle Ages, when several barbarians who worshiped other gods converted to Christianity. There was a mass of conversions. Many of them just exchanged their pagan idols for Christian images. The idea was not to promote idolatry; however, over time this impregnated the church. Instead of worshiping gods, they started to worship the apostles and the mother of Jesus, who became another type of idolatry.

Unfortunately, in many churches in different cultures today, we observe several images and sculptures representing diverse saints replacing God. Originally, they were created to symbolize and help people to remember those important characters. However, as the church was neglecting God's commandment to not make any image or idol, even of God himself (Exodus 20:1–6), the church became a hostage of idolatry. Images of the apostles Peter, Paul, the mother of Jesus, and several others competing in an equal way with reverence for God. Instead of praying only to the Father as Jesus taught (Matthew 6:9–13), people started to pray to Mary and many apostles.

Just as happened in the ancient pagan religions and is still found today in Hinduism and folk beliefs, where each god or entity has a power over something, in these churches it is believed that each saint answers to specific needs. This is not taught by the Bible but is a demonic teaching mixed from different folk religions.

When we observe the different religions of Asia and Africa, we perceive a point in common among them: the gods usually have human characteristics, creating in the people a feeling of identification between their lives and the supernatural. Their gods are as fallen as they are. As in the ancient Greek religion, where the gods betrayed each other and had children with humans that were not their wives, we see the same in other religions today. The Hindu god called Shiva cut off the head of his own son in an act of anger. The god Brahma raped his own daughter Sarasvati. So these gods are merely creations of the human mind corrupted by sin to validate their sinful lifestyle. If you understand the gods of a society, you can understand that society!

Therefore, as you can see, humanity has the habit of creating gods in the image and likeness of man—an attitude opposed to what happened in Genesis 1:26–27. In this way, people try to manipulate these false gods to bless marriages, work, health, and other areas of life, according to their will. Instead of seeking God's will, humanity created gods that satisfy their desires.

In Christian churches, a common mistake is to idolize people. In the biblical narratives, men and women of the past were servants of God. No one would deny Peter's value to the church and his commitment to Christ to the point of being crucified upside down, but Peter was only a man! These men and women were subject to the same temptations and failures as we are.

They were sinners who achieved forgiveness of their sins in Jesus Christ, just as you and I need! See what James wrote in his epistle about the prophet Elijah, who was used powerfully by God in the Old Testament.

> The prayer of a righteous person is powerful and effective. Elijah was a human being, even as we are. He prayed earnestly that it would not rain, and it did

not rain on the land for three and a half years. (James 5:16–17)

Elijah was as human as anyone, but his prayer was answered. What James emphasized was the power of God who answers the prayer, not the supposed power of the servant who asks. The servant is only used by the hands of the Lord. It is in God that we must put our faith! Observe also how James does not ask Elijah in prayer something as if he could hear any prayer. Not even the church, or the synagogues of his time, had images of the prophet Elijah to revere. This was totally unacceptable! Even though he was a great servant of God, Elijah was only a man.

See what happened in the ministry of the apostle Paul and Barnabas. While preaching in the city of Lystra (Acts 14), Paul perceived that a man crippled since birth believed in the message he was preaching. The apostle, with the authority given by Jesus, ordered the paralytic to rise, and before the eyes of the crowd, the man stood up. The astonishment of the city led the crowd to think that Paul and Barnabas were gods who had become men, worshiping them! What a great mistake they made! Look what the apostles did when they saw this happening.

> But when the apostles Barnabas and Paul heard of this, they tore their clothes and rushed out into the crowd, shouting: "Friends, why are you doing this? We too are only human, like you. We are bringing you good news, telling you to turn from these worthless things to the living God, who made the heavens and the earth and the sea and everything in them." (Acts 14:14–15)

Tearing one's clothes was a Jewish practice meaning self-humiliation. "We are also humans like you," they said, making it clear that the healing of that man was God's action, not their own. If the apostles knew what is done today in their names and how they have been divinized and canonized, they would surely rip their clothes again.

Mary is also mistakenly considered immaculate, without sin. This teaching denies what the Word of God teaches. The Bible states that all human beings sinned (Romans 3:10, 23), except Jesus (2 Corinthians 5:18–21; Hebrews 4:15; 1 Peter 2:22). Mary herself said that the Lord was her Savior (Luke 1:47), thereby admitting that she needed to be saved. Jesus was Mary's Savior in the same way that he is ours. She had to believe him as we do! One day when Jesus was teaching his disciples in a house, Mary came outside and asked to speak to him. Look what Jesus stated.

> Who is my mother, and who are my brothers? Pointing to his disciples, he said, "Here are my mother and my brothers. For whoever does the will of my Father in heaven is my brother and sister and mother." (Matthew 12:48–50)

Being the biological mother of Jesus, or his father or his brother, did not make them holy or immaculate. What Jesus declared means that the only way to be part of his holy family is to do the will of God. Because some Jews believed themselves to be special because they were descendants of Abraham, Jesus accused them of hypocrisy; he also wanted to make sure the same confusion should not happen to Mary and his brothers in flesh. Mary was a servant used by God to give birth to Jesus. She was blessed because was chosen, but she was as much a sinner as anyone else. The apostle Paul says,

> For there is one God and one mediator between God and mankind, the man Christ Jesus, who gave himself as a ransom for all people. This has now been witnessed to at the proper time. (1 Timothy 2:5–6)

Paul is ensuring that neither Mary nor Peter, Paul, or anyone else can connect men to God; only Jesus Christ can. No one can listen to or answer our prayers but God himself through Jesus. That is why Jesus taught in the Lord's prayer that we need to pray only to one person, our Heavenly Father, and not to anyone else. Jesus alone lived a sinless life and died for our sins. Only he rose again on the third day, not Peter, Mary, or any other disciple.

Have you ever revered any saint? Have you ever prayed to a man, whether a Christian saint, a Hindu guru, or any spiritual leader who had already died? Have you ever asked Mary or Peter for something? Maybe you even have some "holy" images or objects in your house? How about today confessing to God, repenting, and abandoning each one of these idols? Maybe you did it out of ignorance and you don't feel bad about yourself. But not feeling bad does not change the fact that this is idolatry, and idolatry is a betrayal of God.

Write down the names of saints and people that you have revered, prayed to, or been devoted to. After writing, say the prayer below, quoting each one of the names you wrote. I am sure that God will answer your prayer in grace, freeing you from the evil influences of Satan behind this idolatry pretending to be Christianity. Idolatry is a worthless piece of glass posing as a diamond. Jesus gives us direct access to the Father in a genuine relationship of love and grace, with forgiveness of our sins, honor from above, and inner peace and power from on high. We must never ignore the preciousness of what Jesus conquered for us. Do not believe in the dull glow of the worthless idols created to distract you from the priceless gift of Christ. The truth will set you free!

Names of idols or saints:

_____

_____

_____

> Final prayer:

Lord God Almighty, I confess that I have sinned, idolizing people created by you, worshipping your creation instead of you, Lord. I confess that I have prayed to and revered _____, and I repent of this. Forgive me, Lord! I recognize that only Jesus is Lord, and there is no other besides you!

Day 5

MAGIC AND WITCHCRAFT

In recent years, many fictional movies involving magic have brought to people a new fascination for the occult and witchcraft. The idea of manipulating the supernatural realm to acquire hidden knowledge and power is what magic and witchcraft promise, with an apparent naivety, but the Bible presents them as deadly dangerous. Scriptures do not deny the reality of magic, divination, and witchcraft but explain their true source of power in demons.

As in the Harry Potter's adventures, religions such as Wicca, folk Hinduism, tribal animism, or even Islamic Sufis, millions of people are currently seeking something from demons. Through magic potions, secret phrases, the use of amulets, crystals, herbal mixing, and spirit manipulation, many have sought to control the supernatural. People hardly know that by getting involved with these mystical practices they end up relating to demons, opening their lives to impure spirits. They wish to control the supernatural but end up controlled by it.

Magic and witchcraft are practiced using different names in the world. In Brazil, for example, many Afro Brazilian religions, such as Umbanda, Candomblé, and Quimbanda, practice different types of magic and witchcraft. In Central America, it is found in Voodoo. Europe has also experienced a return to pre-Christian religiosity through different expressions of magic and witchcraft, as found in Wicca, for example. In India, witchcraft is strongly rooted in popular

Hinduism, influencing the animistic rituals of the people in rural areas and even in big cities. Although these bear different names, the idea behind magic and witchcraft is the same. The idea involves controlling the spiritual world through words of power, incantations, mystical ceremonies, special herbs, amulets, and other objects that are believed to possess spiritual power. The key word here is *control,* or manipulate, the spiritual.

When Adam and Eve ate from the forbidden fruit, they did it because they wanted to be like God. Eating the fruit was a way to manipulate the spiritual world to their favor. As Adam's children, we have the same sinful thirst for control and a selfish hunger to be like gods. Magic and witchcraft are different ways of manipulating God, or the spiritual world, to get what we want, no matter what!

When a Christian wears a cord on his arm, or an amulet on his neck, believing that it has magical powers to protect him, he is failing to believe that Jesus is sufficient. Believing in witchcraft means to disbelieve in God. Believing in the power of a cord, an amulet, or a magical charm is disbelieving in the supreme work of Jesus Christ. As Adam and Eve did, those who practice these things are trying to manipulate the spiritual world instead of believing in God's Word.

If you believe in Jesus Christ, you have no reason to be afraid of any spirit, demon, false god, or type of entity. God said to the patriarch Abraham that he would "bless those who bless you, and whoever curses you I will curse" (Genesis 12:3). This means that you don't need to be afraid of any curse or evil eye either because God is enough to protect you, for he needs no amulet to help him.

The practice of magic and witchcraft is ancient, and the Bible does not deny its power but reveals that its source is demonic. Letting yourself be seduced by witchcraft represents associating with demons (Deuteronomy 32:17; 1 Corinthians 10:19–21). These evil spirits deceive people by offering power in exchange for something people want. Presenting themselves as gods, djinns, or even dead people, they deceive many by manipulating people's desire for something.

The involvement with occultism always leads the person to demons, imprisoning the person to some degree. Consulting dead spirits, repeating mantras, invoking an enchantment, and consuming a food or drink consecrated to a spirit are different covenants made with demons. These covenants submit their lives to demon manipulation. See what the Bible says about what King Manasseh did.

> He sacrificed his children in the fire in the Valley of Ben Hinnom, practiced divination and witchcraft, sought omens, and consulted mediums and spiritists. He did much evil in the eyes of the LORD, arousing his anger. (2 Chronicles 33:6)

God clearly commanded his people not to get involved with magic and witchcraft; however, King Manasseh allowed himself to be seduced by them. Read also what God stated to his people in the book of Deuteronomy.

> Let no one be found among you who sacrifices their son or daughter in the fire, who practices divination or sorcery, interprets omens, engages in witchcraft, or casts spells, or who is a medium or spiritist or who consults the dead. Anyone who does these things is detestable to the LORD; because of these same detestable practices the LORD your God will drive out those nations before you. (Deuteronomy 18:10–12)

The words used by God in this text are strong so we can grasp how the Creator feels about these practices. The expression "detestable practices" means that they are repugnant, repulsive to God! The Hebrew word used implies that God wants to vomit when he sees such things being practiced. But read again! It's not only repugnance of what is practiced but also of the person who practices it! People become repulsive because they involve impure spirits.

It is repulsive to God when people seek the reading of fortunes, the prediction of the future by any means, either through coffee grounds in the bottom of a mug or the reading of an animal's viscera. As read in the above verse, God despises divination and forecasts, which are attempts to predict the future. Many people try to read the future by looking to the stars, reading hands, consulting horoscopes, or participating in rituals in forests and temples. Don't be misled by a spirit of divination, because it is the spirit of deceiving!

Only God knows everything, because he is the only one who is omniscient, knowing also the future and all the possible futures. Don't think the future can be predicted by a person or a spirit. When someone asks a demon to predict his future, he is putting his faith in the demonic power, authorizing him to write their future. Through a sinful faith, there is now an alliance between the demon and the person who consulted him. This is why some predictions really happen, because demons received authorization to make them happen.

In Hinduism and African religions, many spiritual entities require certain foods, drinks, sacrifices, and other rituals to fulfill requested desires. These entities are well-known in popular culture, acting in specific areas of life: destruction, revenge, health, marriage, sex, money, power, influence, knowledge, and so on. The false gods Shiva, Vishnu, Kali, Saraswathi, and Lakshmi are just some examples of Hindu names used by demons to enslave people using their desires.

There are many popular beliefs in every society that fit under what the Bible calls witchcraft, and many cultures practice them without awareness of their demonic character. Some traditions have sacred drinks, spiritual potions enchanted for healing. Besides the use of incense to attract good spirits or to repel the evil ones, the use of objects to attract good energies, such as pyramids or crystals, and the use of charms like Buddhist prayers written on a flag enslave people to demonic lies. God requires that we believe only in him, because he is enough!

As described in this chapter, the Word of God clearly condemns the practice of witchcraft and magic in many religions like Islamic Sufism, Jainism, Buddhism, Sikhism, Hinduism, and different forms of animism. The Bible warns that these practices are always involved with demons. Scripture is emphatic in declaring that God has "repugnance" of those who practice such things. In Revelation, God explains what the end for them is.

> But the cowardly, the unbelieving, the vile, the murderers, the sexually immoral, those who practice magic arts, the idolaters and all liars—they will be consigned to the fiery lake of burning sulfur. This is the second death. (Revelation 21:8)

Today you can abandon these practices. You can repent at this very moment, asking God for forgiveness for each of the things you have done. You don't need amulets, potions, enchantments, or any type of magic or witchcraft to be related to the spiritual world. These things claim to mediate between humans and God, but in fact they mediate between humans and Satan. All you need is Jesus.

> For there is one God and one mediator between God and mankind, the man Christ Jesus, who gave himself as a ransom for all people. (1 Timothy 2:5–6)

If you are feeling repugnant in front of God, don't despair! God himself created the way to cleanse you of all impurity, shame, and wickedness, making you a new person: Jesus Christ! Read the following verses and meditate on what God is saying to you!

> But God demonstrates his own love for us in this: While we were still sinners, Christ died for us. (Romans 5:8)

> Now Joshua was dressed in filthy clothes as he stood before the angel.
> The angel said to those who were standing before him, "Take off his filthy clothes." Then he said to Joshua, "See, I have taken away your sin, and I will

put fine garments on you." Then I said, "Put a clean turban on his head." So they put a clean turban on his head and clothed him, while the angel of the LORD stood by. (Zechariah 3:3–5)

But if we walk in the light, as he is in the light, we have fellowship with one another, and the blood of Jesus, his Son, purifies us from all "sin". (1 John 1:7)

This is the moment for you to renounce the impurities you may have practiced through magic and witchcraft. Perhaps you want the help of a Christian brother or sister, if you find it difficult. God gave you brothers and sisters in his church because we need each other to grow together as God's family. While renouncing the practices, do not be afraid, for Christ is greater and infinitely more powerful than any of these powers. This is a day of deliverance!

If you can, find a servant of God (doesn't need to be a pastor), and with him or her (preferably someone of the same gender), make a list of all religious practices you have done and you know are expressions of witchcraft and magic. Besides that, list all the spiritual entities that you have invoked, prayed, worshiped, or somehow related to previously, through spiritual healings, consulting mediums, or any other way. Afterward, pray the following prayer putting in the white space each one of the practices you wrote. Don't worry about how long this may take if you have listed too many. The important thing is to do it with calm and sincerity of heart. Do not only repeat the words, but declare them with all your heart.

> Write.

Dear Lord, I confess that I have been involved with the practice of _____, and I repent! I ask you for forgiveness with all my heart. I renounce

_____ with all my heart in the name of the Lord Jesus Christ. Amen.

Then, for each entity with whom you have related, pray the following prayer with all your heart:

Pray.

Dear Lord, I confess and ask forgiveness for having related to the demon called _____, and I wholeheartedly renounce _____. I order _____ to get out of my life now, in the name of Jesus Christ! My life belongs only to Jesus Christ, and I renounce every evil spirit acting inside me. Come, Jesus, and purify my heart. Come, Jesus, and fill me with your presence!

Day 6

OTHER LIES OF OCCULTISM

One of the most dangerous lies invented by Satan is the teaching of reincarnation and karma. Coming from Eastern religions, such as Hinduism and Buddhism, these doctrines exert great influence in the West through new spiritualist philosophies. These ideas are present in many Hollywood movies, exploring the concepts in different ways. These false teachings are also involved in the new interest in transcendental meditation, yoga, mantras, and the concept of regression to "past lives."

The root of these ideas is the Hindu and Buddhist teaching that life is an eternal cycle whereby you are born and reborn in different forms, receiving in the current life the effects of past ones. For them, the karma is the result, whether positive or negative, individual or collective, that is upon a person.

Reincarnation is the idea that the human spirit after death is reborn in another body that progressively evolves through each reincarnation. These teachings are false because they are the opposite of what the Bible teaches. They are demonic teachings focused on deceiving people. Read what the Bible says about the idea of reincarnation.

> Just as people are destined to die once, and after that
> to face judgment. (Hebrews 9:27)

> As a cloud vanishes and is gone, so one who goes
> down to the grave does not return. He will never
> come to his house again; his place will know him no
> more. (Job 7:9–10)

That is, there is no reincarnation! We die only once, facing judgment right after it. Luke's Gospel, chapter 16, Jesus tells a story to make clear that there are only two destinies for the human being after death: heaven or hell. Jesus speaks of a rich man who is taken immediately to hell when he dies and a beggar who also dies and is immediately taken to heaven. The rich man in torment in hell requests that one of the dead could return to the living ones to warn his family regarding that place, but his request is denied.

With this story, Jesus is warning us that we live only once, making clear that after death are only heaven and hell as possible destinations! Through Jesus's story, the idea of reincarnation is unmasked as a big illusion. Besides, the Catholic teaching of purgatory, as a temporary place where people stay after death to atone for their sins, is also unmasked as another false teaching because the Bible is clear that either the person goes to heaven or to hell; there is no other option! The Bible is even clearer when it speaks about the final judgment.

> Anyone whose name was not found written in
> the book of life was thrown into the lake of fire.
> (Revelation 20:15)

Only those whose names are written in the book of life, which means believers in Jesus Christ, will be saved by God's grace. Those whose names are not found there will be thrown into hell. There is no reincarnation or purgatory!

For many years in India, a country where the majority of people believe in reincarnation, it was possible to witness atrocities because of this demonic belief. Poor parents with babies in their arms threw their children into rivers in the hope that they would reincarnate in a better situation. Men and women in the past laid their heads before giant wooden wheels carrying statues of their idols with a promise that by sacrificing themselves, they would reincarnate in a better life. Even today there are people who sacrifice their newborn babies, believing that they will reincarnate in a better situation. People commit suicide with the hope of reincarnating in a better situation. Dreadful lies preached by demons!

Another dangerous related teaching is the idea of consulting people already dead. The Holy Scriptures do not deny the possibility of talking to spirits but reveal that they are not spirits of dead people but from demons, evil spirits. They deceive people by presenting themselves as the deceased ones. Made vulnerable by the loss of a loved one, many people give themselves over to the illusion of talking to them, not knowing that they are being deceived by very intelligent and convincing demons. Read the following text again:

> Let no one be found among you who sacrifices their son or daughter in the fire, who practices divination or sorcery, interprets omens, engages in witchcraft, or casts spells, or who is a medium or spiritist or who consults the dead. (Deuteronomy 18:10–11)

> When someone tells you to consult mediums and spiritists, who whisper and mutter, should not a people inquire of their God? Why consult the dead on behalf of the living? Consult God's instruction and the testimony of warning. If anyone does not speak according to this word, they have no light of dawn. (Isaiah 8:19–20)

The texts are clear about God's prohibition regarding consulting the dead. Read below some other texts about this.

> Saul died because he was unfaithful to the LORD; he did not keep the word of the LORD and even consulted a medium for guidance, and did not inquire of the

LORD. So the LORD put him to death and turned the
kingdom over to David son of Jesse. (1 Chronicles
10:13–14)

The Spirit clearly says that in later times some will
abandon the faith and follow deceiving spirits and
things taught by demons. (1 Timothy 4:1)

Unfortunately, even some Christians have abandoned the truth
revealed by the Bible, turning to the teachings of demons. Seeking
revelation by consulting the spirits, many people became enslaved
to demons. A brief look at their lives and families can evidence the
oppressive presence of these evil spirits causing dissension, different
sicknesses, mental problems, violence, immorality, and many other
calamities.

I once prayed for the son of a pastor who was secretly going to
a Hindu temple to seek revelation from the spirits. He asked me
to pray for him as he suffered from chronic depression and had
multiple thoughts of suicide. As he prayed, that young man fell
demon possessed. After casting out the demon, I ministered to him
that he had to completely abandon his involvement with those spirits
in order to be totally freed.

If we want to be delivered from Satan's power, we need to be
delivered from his lies! It makes no difference going to the church if
you still believe in Satan's lies that are denounced and repudiated by
the Bible. It is hypocrisy to praise Christ in the church if your heart
is committed to Satan's values. It is like a man who marries a woman
but, in his heart, loves another one. He says that he is committed to his
wife but secretly has an affair with another woman. Unlike a husband
or wife being betrayed, Jesus cannot be deceived because he knows
everything, including the depths of our hearts. Either we give ourselves
completely to him and his Word or we are deceiving ourselves with
demonic lies, living a hypocritical Christianity. It is not the church that
saves you, your Bible opened in your house, or any type of religiosity,
but only surrendering your heart completely to Jesus.

I once met a woman who faithfully followed a Spiritist doctrine and was also attending a church. She declared that for her it was possible to merge the Bible with the idea of reincarnation and the consultation of the dead, affirming that the spirits were good. After showing the texts we read here, opening her eyes that the Bible reveals that these spirits are actually demons, she started to feel bad. She stated that the spirit of a certain doctor, to whom she was relating, was speaking to her at that moment. I laid my hands, as Jesus and the apostles did, and with the authority of the name of Jesus Christ, I commanded the spirit to leave. The demon started to speak through that woman, pretending to be the deceased doctor. I ordered him in Jesus's name to stop the farce and tell who the spirit really was. The demon started to laugh, affirming loudly that he was a demon who was pretending to be that deceased doctor, confessing that for years he had been enslaving that poor woman. I cast out that demon. Afterward the woman gave herself completely to Jesus Christ, abandoning the belief that had imprisoned her for so many years. How about today you break any bond with demons and their false teachings? You can pray the following prayer:

Pray.

Dear Lord, I need your help to remind me of all spiritual involvements I had in my life. Please help me to remember every false teaching that I ever believed, every demonic practice I ever did. Help me to renounce each one of them. I ask you in the name of Jesus Christ. Amen.

Now make a list of every involvement you have had with false teachings and spirits. Practices like the invocation of spirits through pendulum and Ouija board are different ways of the same lies. Hindu mantras that invoke spirits, usually practiced in different types of yoga, are also a type of demonic invocation. These practices open the

lives of practitioners to demon invasion. Beliefs such as reincarnation and karma must also be abandoned completely. Make a list in a paper; take your time. Then make a prayer for each one you wrote.

> List.

Dear Lord, I confess that I have participated in _____, and I renounce with all my heart the lying teachings of _____. Forgive me for this in the name of the Lord Jesus Christ.

Now make a list with the names of the dead people and other spirits you supposedly have related to. Maybe you have already incorporated one of these spirits, just talked to them incorporated in another person, or communicated through a game or another way. The important thing here is to renounce every demon that is behind these spirits. For each name, make the following prayer:

> Pray.

Dear Lord, I confess and ask forgiveness for relating to the demon self-proclaimed _____ and renounce him with all my heart. I order _____ to get out of my life now, in the name of Jesus Christ! I belong only to the Lord Jesus!

Day 7

CLEANING UP

From time to time, everyone needs to clean the house, right? We throw away the garbage we produce, wash the toilet, and vacuum carpets to make everything clean in our homes. After all, we know that an unclean house can harm our health; in addition, it attracts insects and rats. Just as a clean house influences our health and well-being, our spiritual house also needs to be clean.

After considering everything we have seen so far, acknowledging that the religious practices and demonic teachings are disgusting in God's eyes, we need also to clean our houses. This is an important moment in your journey with God, where once and for all you will destroy all religious objects, such as books containing the teachings mentioned above, amulets, holy rocks, spiritual cords, images of idols representing gods and saints, or any other object connected to demonic teachings.

When the apostle Paul lived in the idolatrous city of Ephesus, he preached the Gospel to the people, and many repented and abandoned the teachings of demons. See what they did.

> Many of those who believed now came and openly confessed what they had done. A number who had practiced sorcery brought their scrolls together and burned them publicly. When they calculated the value of the scrolls, the total came to fifty thousand drachmas. (Acts 19:18–19)

This biblical event teaches us some important principles. First, it says that the people who believed openly confessed their sins. Second, they destroyed every scroll, their religious writings, burning them publicly. Let's talk about the first principle! There is immense power when a sinner confesses his sin before men and God, for it requires exposing his true self before all. Confessing is dying, forsaking your false honor by exposing your shame so that Christ can truly cover you with his glory. Pride is the greatest enemy, seeking to hide behind a self-illusion.

God does not require sacrifices of animals or anything else, for Jesus's sacrifice was enough to forgive us and restore our relationship with him. However, we are called to offer ourselves as a sacrifice before him, truly dying in Christ. In order to have new life in Christ, we must die to our present life, where confession and repentance is the beginning of this process. Read what the scripture says about this.

> Then he (Jesus) said to them all: "Whoever wants to be my disciple must deny themselves and take up their cross daily and follow me. For whoever wants to save their life will lose it, but whoever loses their life for me will save it. What good is it for someone to gain the whole world, and yet lose or forfeit their very self? Whoever is ashamed of me and my words, the Son of Man will be ashamed of them when he comes in his glory and in the glory of the Father and of the holy angels." (Luke 9:23–26)

> We are those who have died to sin; how can we live in it any longer? Or don't you know that all of us who were baptized into Christ Jesus were baptized into his death? We were therefore buried with him through baptism into death in order that, just as Christ was raised from the dead through the glory of the Father, we too may live a new life. (Romans 6:2–4)

> Therefore, I urge you, brothers and sisters, in view of
> God's mercy, to offer your bodies as a living sacrifice,
> holy and pleasing to God—this is your true and proper
> worship. (Romans 12:1)

Confessing and repenting of our sins is indispensable for our deliverance. This is how we die to ourselves and to the world. We cannot clean our inner home without repentance and confession! See what James says about confessing sins to one another.

> Therefore, confess your sins to each other and pray for
> each other so that you may be healed. The prayer of a
> righteous person is powerful and effective. (James 5:16)

Openly confessing our sins to a brother or a sister is liberating, for it breaks the spiritual bonds holding us. When we confess to God, we are forgiven, but when we confess to a brother, we are delivered! Confessing involves cutting the bond of pride that controls sin in our lives.

Many people in Asia and Africa, living in cultures shaped by honor and shame, are afraid of publicly confessing their sins. For them, worse than sinning is the shame of someone finding out what they have done! But it is necessary to look at this text written by James and rely on the certainty that confession to God, and to some mature brother or sister, draws the power of hidden sin from our hearts. There is healing! You don't need to confess to everyone but to someone or some mature brothers who can pray for you and follow up. When we walk together in transparency with loving brothers and sisters, we are supported and grow spiritually.

In the previous chapters, you were challenged to abandon idolatry and confess sins of witchcraft, magic, and false teachings. However, maybe you are still hiding something and do not have the courage to confess. Perhaps it is something so significant in your life that you have buried it deeply in your heart, with no desire to relive it. Nevertheless, the guilt, fear, shame, and anger corroding you from inside are inducing in you the false self-image that you chose to promote to others, at the cost of your integrity in front of God. These anguishes will never leave you until you confess and abandon these sins, taking possession of the forgiveness that Jesus Christ offers! To put on the glorious vestments of holiness provided by Jesus, you must first put off the garments of shame. Confession cleans the inner house!

The second important principle is that the people of Ephesus brought their books of occultism to be burned because they realized they were dangerous and demonic. Every book that teaches witchcraft, magic, incantations, spirit invocation, sorcery, divination, and objects with spiritual meanings like amulets, pyramids, spiritual cords, idols, images of gurus, saints, or any worshiped leader fits this description and must be destroyed.

Once a woman asked me if she could give to someone her books of witchcraft, instead of destroying them. I asked, "If you found drugs in your house, would you give them to someone? Would you give drugs as a gift to someone?" "No! Of course not!" she answered. Just as drugs are dangerous, these objects and books are also dangerous and need to be destroyed. They are even more dangerous than drugs! They must not be sold or donated but destroyed! She soon understood and burned the books.

Perhaps you have in your house some image of someone considered holy, and this image has an emotional value. However, imagine if a married man, soon after the wedding, discovers that his wife possesses some pictures of another man, someone she loved, keeping them affectionately in a certain drawer. How would he feel? Nobody will say, "It is just a photo, no problem," because it is evident that those pictures are emotional links in the wife's heart. Similarly, God does not want any emotional link between his children and false gods, gurus, saints, or other demonic powers represented by any idols.

James 4:5 says that God is "jealous" of us, and he requests total fidelity. Either God is unique and enough for us, or he is not our God. Either he is everything, or he is nothing for us! Many choose to stay with the image and do not realize that God is not present in his home.

In the Old Testament, we read interesting stories of God asking for the destruction of images and altars built to the idols. In Judges 6, God appeared to Gideon when the people of Israel were away from the Lord, being oppressed by many enemies. God told Gideon that he would free the people, but first he needed to destroy the altars built by his family to other gods. After Gideon struck down the altars, God used him powerfully to release all the people. In 2 Kings 22–23, we read the story of the King Josiah, who at a young age rediscovered the book of God's law hidden in the temple, which no one had read for many years. By reading it, he discovered how God despised idolatry. Josiah humbled himself before the Lord, destroying all images and altars and demolishing everything that God declared he abhorred. Because of this act of obedience, God powerfully blessed the nation during Josiah's time!

And you, do you have altars in your house? Are there images of saints, Mary, or any idols or other gods? Perhaps a statue of Ganesh, Buddha, or another false divinity? Maybe a book of magic, witchcraft, Islam Sufism, Hinduism, spiritism, or something similar? Possibly a picture of a guru or another self-declared divine person? These are all altars raised to false gods in your home and you must destroy them! At this moment, with courage and faith in Christ, I invite you to destroy these things before God in an attitude of worship, declaring that Jesus Christ is your only Lord and Savior! Do not throw them in the garbage or sell them to someone. Burn them while you pray to the Lord in an attitude of praise, devoting yourself fully to the only and true God. This is the day you will clean your house of any spiritual dirty!

> Pray together with someone.

Lord Jesus, today I destroy each one of these items before the Lord. Just as Gideon knocked down the

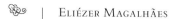

altars and consecrated himself to the Lord, I now destroy these idols, books, and objects, confessing that they were altars that I raised in my life. Today I sanctify my life and my house to you. Accept this as an expression of worship to you, Lord! Amen!

Day 8

SYMPTOMS OF OPPRESSION

The first thing doctors do when someone goes to the hospital is to understand the symptoms of the patient. The symptoms may help him identify the disease, in order to administer the correct treatment. Spiritually it is also possible to identify symptoms of oppression and even demonic possession. While oppression is the external pressure caused by Satan and his demons over someone, possession involves his control inside. A Christian can still be oppressed, but not possessed, because the true Christian is sealed with the Holy Spirit, as the apostle Paul says in Ephesians 1:13.

In this chapter, we will identify different symptoms; some even reveal demonic infections. Nobody likes to know that they are afflicted by demons. But imagine if you had a cancer that can be treated. Wouldn't you like to find out as soon as possible, to treat it? Or would you rather ignore it and suffer for years until you die of the disease? No matter what symptoms you have, there is a solution for your problem: Jesus Christ! Let's study some biblical texts that will help us identify the main symptoms.

> When Jesus got out of the boat, a man with an impure spirit came from the tombs to meet him. This man lived in the tombs, and no one could bind him anymore, not even with a chain. For he had often been chained hand and foot, but he tore the chains apart and broke the irons on his feet. No one was

strong enough to subdue him. Night and day among the tombs and in the hills he would cry out and cut himself with stones. (Mark 5:2–5)

This is the story of the Gadarene, a man afflicted by many demons, finding deliverance when he met Jesus!

First Symptom: Desire to Live Alone

The Gadarene lived in the tombs, for demons always lead people to self-isolation! People influenced by demons prefer to live alone, far from everyone. They stay away from people because they hurt everyone around them. Influenced by demons, people slowly become unwanted and rejected by those they hurt. Sometimes, influenced by guilt or shame, they abandon friends and family; at other times, influenced by anger and fear, they are rejected by them. Satan always aims at the isolation of people, sometimes exploiting pride, other times self-esteem. Isolated, the individual is an easy prey to Satan!

Alone, separated from society and family, the individual is dehumanized. Satan brutalizes people, fragmenting them from inside, destroying God's image. Aiming to make people after his own demonic image, Satan leads them to grotesque behaviors. Alone, people are unable to love and be loved. Alone, people are controlled by selfishness, becoming vulnerable to demonic illusions and overwhelming vices. Alone, isolated from others, people become vulnerable to madness, becoming similar to the Gadarene.

I still remember a lady brought to me for prayer in a village in India. She was disconnected from reality and considered mentally ill by the local people. I remember that, by praying, many demons shook her body, taking her to the ground violently. After we cast out the demons, she became totally conscient, asking why she was in that place. Her madness was demonic, but that day, she met Jesus, who delivered her completely!

One more thing that is important to say is that even though Satan leads many people to loneliness and, with time, to madness, it is incorrect to affirm that every madness is caused by demons. There are psychopathologies that require the assistance of psychologists and psychiatrists. Discernment for each case is essential!

Second Symptom: The Exterior World Reflects the Interior World!

The Gadarene chose to live in the tombs because it was the place that most reflected his inner world, his interiority. The grave reflected his heart. Demons always lead people to places that reflect their evil and unclean nature. If not a graveyard, demons many times lead people to live in brothels, drug houses, bars, or somewhere created to degrade the human being, extracting all the life, joy, and beauty given by God. As in the story of the prodigal son told by Jesus (Luke 15:11–32), many lost sons of God are led by Satan to live among pigs.

I met people infected by demons where their houses were too dirty, with trash everywhere. A certain house I visited had so many rats and cockroaches with dirty clothes on the floor and garbage in several places, but the woman living there did not care. No wonder demons are called dirty spirits. They transform the place where they are or lead people to places that reflect their nature. The woman living in that house was demon possessed, and after experiencing deliverance of the spirits, and giving her life to Jesus, she became a new woman. Her house, even though simple and poor, became clean and pretty. Her outer world was affected by her inner world! How is your external world? Does it reveal something of your interiority?

Third Symptom: Violence

Scripture says that no one could bind the Gadarene. Even in chains, he would break them. His strength and violence were extreme. The demons exerted their total control and power through that man. Some violence is always present when demons operate!

The greater the degree of demonic infection, the greater the violence. Verbal, physical, sexual violence, abuse, irritability, anger without measure, robbery, kidnapping, death, and rape are common fruits of those influenced by demons. While some are influenced by demons to the level of uncontrollably hurting their loved ones, others are so dominated that they realize terrible acts. I remember expelling the demons of a small, skinny girl who could lift with her hands two tall and strong men. They were unable to control her. Only after expelling her demons, that girl become docile. Human force is incapable of subduing demonic power and violence. Only the power of Jesus can control violent people and bring peace to their heart. Are you a violent person? Can you control your anger, or are you controlled by it?

Fourth Symptom: Self-Hurting

The biblical narrative also says that the Gadarene cut himself with stones and cried out day and night. Can you imagine the suffering this man was experiencing? He was self-mutilating, which is a strong symptom of demonic influence.

Usually, self-mutilation begins with thoughts like *I am useless. Life has no meaning. I hate myself.* Then it develops into physical acts. It may seem strange, but Satan makes the person seek relief from his anguish by cutting and hurting himself. This usually happens with people who are isolated, as was the case of the Gadarene. The person puts in himself the focus of everything and therefore expresses his guilt, anger, and shame upon his own soul and body. The violence he inflicted upon others is inflicted upon himself. He feels bad and alleviated at the same time. He experiences pain and pleasure in an endless, vicious cycle. A demonic cycle!

Another typical way of self-hurting includes the psychosomatic diseases. They are not consciously inflicted upon the body but are caused subconsciously by our inner anguishes. Sometimes they are caused by demonic influence, but most of the time, they are caused by our inability to solve our own sins. Guilt, shame, pathologic fear, and anger are redirected inwardly, causing different sicknesses. Instead of putting our sins upon the sacrifice of Jesus, we redirect them inwardly. Some of the consequences are anxiety, irritability, depression, exhaustion, constant headaches, stomach pains, frequent bouts of diarrhea, accelerated heartbeat, constant allergies, joint pain, and many others, possible diseases caused by our own self-aggression.

People suffering from psychosomatic diseases are not cutting themselves with rocks but with their anxieties caused by sin!

About this, the apostle Peter wrote, "Cast all your anxiety on him because he cares for you" (1 Peter 5:7). We need to change the focus on ourselves by pouring our anxieties on Jesus!

Fifth Symptom: Loss of Shame

After Jesus expelled the demons, the Gadarene got dressed (Mark 5:15); after all, he was naked. This is another symptom of a person infected by demons: lack of shame.

Shame is slowly lost when Satan isolates the person, making him focused only on himself. Sometimes the person is isolated, even though apparently surrounded by people. First, we stop loving God, then we stop loving others; with time, we also stop loving ourselves. This is part of Satan's process of dehumanization, destroying the image of God in human beings. The lack of shame paves the broad road that leads people to self-destruction. Meditate on the following words of Jesus:

> So in everything, do to others what you would have them do to you, for this sums up the Law and the Prophets. "Enter through the narrow gate. For wide is the gate and broad is the road that leads to destruction, and many enter through it. But small is the gate and narrow the road that leads to life, and only a few find it." (Matthew 7:12–14)

The narrow gate is entered by faith and love, for love sums up God's law. The road to God is true love. But the road to destruction is the highway of indifference, the road of shame. The shameless one became unable to see himself through the eyes of God and other people.

Slowly the person becomes indifferent to his own spiritual life, consequently indifferent to others. He or she becomes increasingly self-centered, focused on his or her desires, sufferings, and will.

There is nobody else in the world suffering or in need, only himself or herself! The person slowly learns to ignore the will of others, their opinions, needs, and eyes of reproach. When one becomes unable to see oneself through the eyes of others, whether because one is incapable or because one doesn't care, shame is lost!

A person without shame sees his body as an object, a tool used for self-satisfaction. The shameless can see other people as mere objects to be used, where their value is measured by the satisfaction that they can provide. This can be perceived in people who enjoy showing off their nudity to others, also present in the use of sensual clothes to seduce. The higher the level of sexual immorality, the higher the lack of shame. The only thing that matters is the self!

People without shame use dirty, immoral, and pornographic words. People influenced by demons usually curse others, complain all the time, swear, and don't stop behaving like this in front of others, even children. Look what Jesus said about this.

> A good man brings good things out of the good stored up in his heart, and an evil man brings evil things out of the evil stored up in his heart. For the mouth speaks what the heart is full of. (Luke 6:45)

In other words, the mouth reveals the heart! You can see that there are different levels of degradation. The Gadarene was totally controlled by demons for he was possessed by a legion of demons; therefore, he was walking around naked. Even though we can find some people today possessed as the Gadarene was, living totally under the control of demons, most people are influenced to a lesser degree yet still under Satan's power! Is there any area in your life where you have been living shamelessly?

Shame is a problem of the heart. Only when we learn to love God with all our strength can we become able to love our neighbor and thus love ourselves in the right way. Only love realized through loving God and the neighbor is genuinely self-love, the single cure for shame. Only Jesus can change our shameless nakedness, clothing us in robes of holy love!

These symptoms help us to identify whether we are being influenced by demons or not. Have you identified yourself with any of them or maybe more than one? This is an important time for you to find a servant of God, a brother or sister in Christ, to help you confess your sins to Jesus, asking for his healing.

> Therefore, confess your sins to each other and pray for each other so that you may be healed. The prayer of a righteous person is powerful and effective. (James 5:16)

Select the sins you need to confess, or write others not highlighted here.

idolatry	pornography	betrayal	adultery
sensuality	homosexuality	greed	selfishness
pride	prejudice	racism	theft
manipulation	lying	omission	indifference
incredulity	attachment to money	hypocrisy	cowardice
murder	violence	cursing	self-aggression
bitterness	arrogance	swearing	self-mutilation
sexual immorality	addictions	drugs	

For each selected item, make a prayer like this with a brother in Christ:

> Pray.

Lord Jesus, I confess that I sinned when I did
_____. I repent and ask your forgiveness
in the name of the Lord Jesus Christ. Amen!

Day 9

WHOSE FAULT IS IT?

Do you consider yourself a blessed or cursed person? Many people believe that we have inherited from our parents the guilt of the mistakes they made. Some Christians even teach this, based on a misreading of Exodus 20:5–6. See what the Bible says.

> I, the LORD your God, punishing the children for the sin of the parents to the third and fourth generation of those who hate me, but showing love to a thousand generations of those who love me and keep my commandments. (Exodus 20:5–6)

Do we really inherit sins from our parents and grandparents? Is God blaming me for sins that I have never committed but that my great-grandfathers did? Certainly, this is not what the Bible is saying! What God is saying is that the consequences of our sins affect our children and grandchildren. This does not mean that they inherit our guilt and sins as if some karmic law controlled our history. God is warning us that our sins have consequences on the next generations!

When we look back at our parents and grandparents, we may be able to identify several sins that they committed that damaged us. Some of these sins even motivated us to repeat them. Their sins influenced the corruption of our hearts. However, our sins were always our own decisions!

It is not uncommon to see whole families repeating the same

patterns of sin and iniquity. Promiscuous mothers with promiscuous daughters. Violent fathers with violent sons. Addicted parents with addicted children. The truth is not that the son inherits from his father some demon that forces him to do the same but that the son suffers the consequence of the father's sins, many times learning to commit the same ones.

But make no mistake: the fault for the sins you have committed is yours and yours alone, although you may have been hurt and deeply influenced by your family in the past. The decision is personal, but the consequences affect others.

When the people of Israel were in the Babylonian captivity, they used to say that their "parents have eaten sour grapes, and the children's teeth are set on edge" (Jeremiah 31:29). They implied that they were suffering the guilt for the sins committed by their parents, and not because of their owns. But God, through the prophet Ezekiel, declared,

> What do you people mean by quoting this proverb about the land of Israel: "The parents eat sour grapes, and the children's teeth are set on edge"? As surely as I live, declares the Sovereign LORD, you will no longer quote this proverb in Israel. (Ezekiel 18:2–3)

In the whole chapter of Ezekiel 18, God describes that if the son of an unjust man decides to obey him, he will not be condemned. But if the son of a righteous man decides to live unjustly, God will condemn him. For every soul is responsible for itself! One day we will give account before the divine court, not of the acts of our grandparents and parents but of our own acts! We can't blame others for what we have done.

When Eve was tempted by Satan, she decided to believe the serpent and disbelieve God! God told that if they ate that fruit they would die, but the serpent said they would be like God. Similarly, today, even if deceived by Satan, influenced by demons, or with sins learned from our parents and grandparents, the mistakes and sins we make are personal decisions we do before God. One day we will give an account of all this before him!

A good example that shows that we do not inherit the guilt, or any curse from our parents, is the story of Cain and Abel, narrated in Genesis 4. Both inherited the consequences of the sins committed by their parents, being born outside the Garden, needing to work. But they did not inherit their guilt! When Abel brought a sacrifice to God, it was accepted and considered righteous (Matthew 23:35; Hebrews 11:4). But Cain did not bring a pleasant sacrifice perhaps because it was not a sincere expression of worship. His sacrifice was not accepted; consequently, moved by jealous, he killed his own brother. Cain was not compelled by the sins inherited from Adam and Eve but made a personal decision. Therefore, we can see two brothers following two different outcomes of blessing or curse.

Jesus offers us forgiveness and salvation for all our sins. He offers us not because we deserve it but because he loves us. However, forgiveness involves repentance and confession. If we do not admit our sins and instead justify ourselves or project the responsibility on our parents or other people, then we can't experience forgiveness and deliverance.

This is the danger of the false teachings regarding hereditary curses or the law of karma. These teachings lead us to hold others accountable and prevent us from assuming our responsibilities! Many psychoanalysts today also fall into this trap, leading people to negate their responsibility by projecting it onto others, whether other people or biological impulses, social problems, or other factors. These facts are indeed important, and they influence us, but the Bible calls us to embrace our self-responsibility in order to be saved.

We must look sincerely in the mirror of our soul to see who we really are so that without restrictions, we admit our greatest mistakes, faults, and sins before the Lord. Only when we realize that we are unworthy can we be forgiven.

The fact that we have been influenced by our parents, or by the family or social environment in which we are involved, does not exempt us from our responsibility. Jesus is the perfect proof. He lived in a world corrupted by sin, was tempted in every way, but never sinned. You and I are responsible for our sins!

Many people try to justify their actions before God. Nevertheless, only one person is able to justify us in the divine court: Jesus Christ! It is Jesus who makes us worthy. "For all those who exalt themselves will be humbled, and those who humble themselves will be exalted" (Luke 14:11). How about today admitting the sins you have committed before God? How about today confessing the sins that until now you have projected on others as an excuse? How about today assuming the deeper truths of your sins, coming out of the denial behind which you've been hiding?

It is true that we must be aware of the sins of our parents and grandparents because they have influenced our choices. Often we do not realize how influenced we have been by attitudes, beliefs, words of curses, and cultural sins. People frequently transform the sins of their parents into their own. Sons who have watched their fathers beat their mothers grow up and often start beating their wives. Mothers who use their bodies to manipulate men eventually produce daughters who do the same. Rejected people tend to become rejecters. Abused people often become abusers. Hurt individuals tend to hurt others. The perpetual cycle ends only when the individual meets Jesus, assumes his responsibility, and repents!

In the Old Testament was an interesting practice of confessing the sins of the parents before God. This practice was instructive, bringing to light some principles.

- Sins have consequences for others.
- If we repeat them, we become as guilty as our parents.
- Maybe we have already followed their sinful examples and must repent of these sins.

Ezekiel 18 throws light on this spiritual truth. It is good to identify the sins of our parents and grandparents, not to blame them and absolve us from our responsibility but to understand what influences were upon us to sin. Were they violent? Was blood spilled by someone in the family? Were they promiscuous? Is there a history of betrayal? Are there any reports of suicide in the family? Knowing your family's history of sins can shed light on why you have behaved the way you have. You are not a victim of your environment, because Jesus wants to set you free! Jesus can once and for all break the cycle of sinful and demonic influence in your life!

Look at your family and social environment and write on a paper the sins you have learned from them. Try to spend some time thinking about what you need to admit without justifying or blaming anyone. After that, pray confessing each sin, admitting your guilt and responsibility. Ask God for forgiveness in Jesus's name for each one of them and trust that he is forgiving you!

> Come near to God and he will come near to you. Wash your hands, you sinners, and purify your hearts, you double-minded. Grieve, mourn and wail. Change your laughter to mourning and your joy to gloom. Humble yourselves before the Lord, and he will lift you up. (James 4:8–10)

Make a chart like this on a sheet of paper. Pray asking God for wisdom to discern which sins you learned from your father and which you learned from your mother. Then pray at the end for each item written.

Write.

Sins learned from father	Sins learned from mother

> Pray.

Lord Jesus, I confess that I learned from my _____ the sin of _____. I admit and repent of practicing this, and I ask your forgiveness. I forgive my _____ for having influenced me to do this. In Jesus's name, amen!

Day 10

THE RIGHT IMAGE OF GOD

When God gave to Moses the famous Ten Commandments inscribed on a stone, one of the least understood commandments today is the following:

> You shall not misuse the name of the LORD your God, for the LORD will not hold anyone guiltless who misuses his name. (Exodus 20:7)

Misusing God's name is more than just playing with it. It is disrespecting God's holiness. We must consciously avoid cursing or swearing because they usually involve God's name in disrespectful or meaningless contexts. We throw his name in the mud when we do this. However, there are other ways of misusing the name of the Lord.

We misuse his name when we create in our minds a distorted image of who he is, when we blame him for things that happened to us in the past, or when we attribute to him the responsibility of our mistakes. We take his name in vain when we disrespect his justice and holiness, excusing ourselves using God's mercy, affirming proudly that he will always forgive us.

I met a woman who was sexually abused by her grandfather when she was a child. As she was hurt by a man, she grew up looking at men in an increasingly distorted way. She learned to despise them without realizing that she was doing this because of her terrible experience. Her abuse became her lens through which to see the world. She gradually became resistant to God, mainly because the Bible calls him the Father. She could not respect or accept any love from this God presented with masculine characteristics. That woman couldn't believe that God was good and really loves people. Her distorted vision of a father did not allow her to see the true Father that God is and wants to be for all of us. The woman unconsciously blamed every man and God. Her distorted view of God and of all men made her live imprisoned in the abuse she had suffered. She was still trapped in that violent space. She became an embittered person, difficult to relate to, and was eventually abandoned by her whole family. She became lonely and started thinking about suicide!

The road for her deliverance and complete transformation was long, but it began with the correct perception of who God really is. She met the Heavenly Father. She learned that what had happened to her was a terrible sin caused by her grandfather, not by every man, and definitely not by God. By understanding that it was precisely because of these sins that Jesus Christ came into the world, and by trusting in his plans, that woman was touched by Jesus's power.

Jesus is the perfect expression of God's love and justice; he was sent to bring mercy to those who believe and judgment to those who do not. Trusting in his love and resting in his righteousness was the path she took, finding rest for the suffering she had experienced since childhood.

Have you misused God's name? Does the mental image you have of the Lord match with what the Bible says? Let's see what the Bible reveals about who God really is! Please meditate carefully on each text quoted below. God's Word is powerful enough to speak directly to you!

1. There is only one God. He is the Creator of everything, and he deserves our worship!
   You are worthy, our Lord and God, to receive glory and honor and power, for you created all things, and by your will they were created and have their being. (Revelation 4:11)

The sea is his, for he made it, and his hands formed the dry land. (Psalm 95:5)

2. Only the Creator should be worshiped!

   You shall not make for yourself an image in the form of anything in heaven above or on the earth beneath or in the waters below. (Exodus 20:4)

3. God is the source of his own existence!

   For as the Father has life in himself, so he has granted the Son also to have life in himself. (John 5:26)

4. God never changes!

   I the LORD do not change. (Malachi 3:6)

   Every good and perfect gift is from above, coming down from the Father of the heavenly lights, who does not change like shifting shadows. (James 1:17)

5. God is eternal!

   Before the mountains were born or you brought forth the whole world, from everlasting to everlasting you are God. (Psalm 90:2)

6. God is omnipresent; he is everywhere!

   Who can hide in secret places so that I cannot see them? declares the LORD. Do not I fill heaven and earth? declares the LORD. (Jeremiah 23:24)

7. God is omniscient; he knows all things!

    You have searched me, LORD, and you know me. You know
    when I sit and when I rise; you perceive my thoughts from
    afar. You discern my going out and my lying down; you are
    familiar with all my ways. Before a word is on my tongue
    you, LORD, know it completely. You hem me in behind and
    before, and you lay your hand upon me. Such knowledge
    is too wonderful for me, too lofty for me to attain. (Psalm
    139:1–6)

8. God is omnipotent; everything is possible for God!

    With God, everything is possible. (Matthew 19:2)

9. God is holy; he cannot lie or do evil!

    Be holy, because I am holy. (1 Peter 1:16)

    It is impossible for God to lie. (Hebrews 6:18)

    When tempted, no one should say, "God is tempting me." For
    God cannot be tempted by evil, nor does he tempt anyone.
    (James 1:13)

10. God is the righteous Judge!

    Now there is in store for me the crown of righteousness,
    which the Lord, the righteous Judge, will award to me on
    that day—and not only to me, but also to all who have longed
    for his appearing. (2 Timothy 4:8)

11. God is good!

    No one is good—except God alone. (Mark 10:18)

12. Jesus Christ is God who became man!

> The Word became flesh and made his dwelling among us. We have seen his glory, the glory of the one and only Son, who came from the Father, full of grace and truth. (John 1:14)

13. Jesus is the only way to God!

> I am the way and the truth and the life. No one comes to the Father except through me. (John 14:6)

14. Jesus died on the cross because of you!

> But God demonstrates his own love for us in this: While we were still sinners, Christ died for us. (Romans 5:8)

> For God so loved the world that he gave his one and only Son, that whoever believes in him shall not perish but have eternal life. (John 3:16)

15. God wants to bless those who seek him by faith!

> And without faith it is impossible to please God, because anyone who comes to him must believe that he exists and that he rewards those who earnestly seek him. (Hebrews 11:6)

Maybe you are like that woman I mentioned. Maybe your abuse was different, but you, like her, developed a distorted image of God. Today, he wants you to know him for real. Maybe you are still in that place where you were deeply hurt and can't get out of there by your own strength. But God is the perfect, omnipotent, omniscient, and omnipresent Father who loves you completely. He has the power to get you out of any room of suffering!

If you ask him, Jesus will enter this place of pain with you and stretch out his hand to take you out, forever! When you see Jesus standing in your place of sorrow, you can look at his hands and perceive the holes. He carries in his own body the mark of his love for you and me—the marks of the sins committed against you in that dark place! Jesus is the only one who can get you out of this room! He wants to be your true Savior and Lord. With a penetrating look, he offers his right hand with a smile in his face. So why don't you stretch your own hand and surrender right now? Why don't you trust him and leave this place for good? Yes, I know this is a spiritual exercise we are doing here, but I am really inviting you to see him with your eyes of faith and physically express this by stretching your hand to Jesus! Let him take your pains today, judge your unjudged causes, and give you peace. Perhaps you need to confess your distorted concepts of him. Maybe you just need to cry in front of him. Enjoy this moment with Jesus. Cry, confess, and surrender yourself; however, in the end, take Jesus's hand and leave this room and never come back!

Day 11

THE LORD IS MY SHEPHERD

One of the most famous psalms in the Bible is undoubtedly Psalm 23. Written by David, this poem brings deep and rich principles to our souls. As a shepherd, David knew well the pastoral context in which he wrote. He began his poetic statement by placing himself as a sheep before the divine shepherd. He wrote, "The LORD is my shepherd, I lack nothing." What a profound statement; after all, for God to be our shepherd, we must place ourselves as his sheep! Of all the animals that can be domesticated, the sheep is one of the most obedient and submissive! Our relationship with God needs to be built on our submission, surrendering ourselves to him, understanding that he wants the best for us. A good part of the anguish that plagues our hearts is tied to the lack of submission we have categorically disposed against the Lord. We can only say that we "lack nothing" if God is indeed our shepherd!

Jesus stated that his sheep hear his voice and follow him (John 10:27). Have you heard the Lord's voice? Are you intentionally obeying or resisting him? Are there any areas in your life that you have not yet surrendered to Christ? You need to surrender every area of your life, becoming a sheep so that Jesus can guide you as your shepherd!

David declared with conviction, "I lack nothing," for he knows that God, as a good shepherd, will never let his flock be deprived of its needs. The shepherd was concerned to supply the needs of the sheep. Therefore, we can also pray and ask our good shepherd, knowing that he takes care of us. Jesus himself encourages us to pray by asking,

> So I say to you: Ask and it will be given to you; seek and you will find; knock and the door will be opened to you. For everyone who asks receives; the one who seeks finds; and to the one who knocks, the door will be opened. (Luke 11:9–10)

Jesus affirmed that we should seek first the kingdom of God, his will, explaining that it is God himself who takes care of supplying our needs (Matthew 6:31–34). We can ask God knowing that he desires to reward us (Hebrews 11:6). Besides, we must remember that he makes no distinction between people, not choosing some over others (Acts 10:34). You are no less important than any other son or daughter! In the Lord's Prayer, the Lord teaches us to boldly say, "Give us today our daily bread" (Matthew 6:11). We can confidently ask him to meet our daily needs.

Perhaps you wonder why our prayers are often not answered. Why do we ask and the Lord does not answer or looks like he did not answer? We can think about three possible answers for this question. First, it is possibly not the right time to receive what we asked from the Lord. Sometimes we are like children asking the father for a gift that we are not ready to receive. We need maturity before receiving some of our requests. That is why many times God makes us wait, even though we don't understand why. Abraham waited many years before God fulfilled his promise, giving him a son. God knows the right moment for everything!

The second reason is that we presume that God did not answer when in fact we never truly heard any answer from God. There is a big difference! Sometimes Christians pray without even expecting any answer from God. These are mere religious prayers. We presume God's answers are negative because we never heard any. When God answers, he can say yes, no, or wait. But he answers! When the prophet Elijah prayed, asking for rain in Israel, he did not have any answer immediately (1 Kings 18:43). He prayed again and again, sending his servant to look toward the sea, searching for any clouds. He did this seven times until he saw a small cloud, which was a sign that God had answered positively! How many times did you just give up praying? Do not presume that God said no, unless you heard him say so. Pray until you receive his answer!

The third reason why sometimes our prayers are not answered is that our requests are selfish, greedy fruits not of our real need but of our vanity. James wrote about this.

> When you ask, you do not receive, because you ask with wrong motives, that you may spend what you get on your pleasures. (James 4:3)

Have you been asking the Lord motivated by your needs or by your pleasures? Understanding that God always supplies our needs is liberating! Equally, denying our fleshly impulses that lead us to desire what we don't really need is also liberating! Self-denial sets us free from the oppressive lordship of our sinful flesh, for by faith we submit ourselves to the gracious lordship of the good shepherd Jesus. After all, it was the good shepherd who said, "Deny yourself" (Matthew 16.24).

When the Lord is our shepherd, we can truly rest. We know that God is guiding us toward green pastures and quiet waters (Psalm 23:2). Rest is the destination, but also the path by which we get there! The Lord guides us "to quiet waters" (Psalm 23:2), but we are also guided quietly, calmly! Our path should not be crossed eagerly, anxiously, without peace. The way our heavenly shepherd guides us through this life is a gentle and calm one. Even if we face obstacles and difficulties because we are not free of suffering and challenges, we take quiet and confident steps following the shepherd who walks with us side by side. As Moses also wrote about rest, "Whoever dwells in the shelter of the Most High will rest in the shadow of the Almighty" (Psalm 91:1). Resting is not only the destination but a new lifestyle we need to learn!

Unfortunately, many of us walk anxiously, influenced by countless fears, anxieties, and worries. In Psalm 23, we are invited by David, who was a king with many responsibilities and worries, to put off our royal garments, our arrogance, presumptions, and restlessness, to humble ourselves to the point of becoming a sheep. Our good shepherd invites us to abandon the desire for control. There is no reason for fear when the Lord is our shepherd or reason for anxiety when we are guided by the one who knows all things.

David affirmed that the Lord is guiding us gently into "quiet waters" and not troubled or agitated. Troubled waters pose a danger to the sheep, for when they bend over to drink, they become vulnerable to be dragged by the current. Every shepherd knows that these waters are dangerous. We need to remember that sheep are usually clumsy and that they are walking sponges! Being swept away by the current could be fatal! That's why the shepherd had to take his sheep over hills and across plains to find calm waters.

Now imagine that during one of these days of walking, after a long time under the hot sun, and naturally becoming very thirsty, the sheep saw in the distance a beautiful river with crystal-clear water running violently through the countryside. The frantic water of the river is dangerous for her, but the sheep does not realize the danger because she is driven by her thirst. That is why she rushes blindly toward the waters until she hears her shepherd's voice calling her back to the safe path. Obedient that she is, she resists her thirst, discards the vision of what would apparently satisfy her need, and turns to her shepherd. After all, the shepherd knows his sheep and never lets any of them succumb to thirst on the way. The shepherd always takes care of the flock's needs! The sheep knows that it is worth waiting with thirst because soon she will reach safe waters.

What about you? Have you heard the voice of the good shepherd calling you, or have you been carried by the currents of a desire that has overwhelmed you? When Jesus met the Samaritan woman at a well in Samaria, he showed her that only he could quench her thirst! The story is told in John 4. Jesus said that he was the fountain of living water, the only source that could quench her existential thirst.

Jesus helped the woman to see that her spiritual thirst was expressed in the fact that she was with her fifth man, and that even he was not her husband. She was thirsty to be loved, and as she sought to be quenched in those men, she was engulfed by her longing, yielding to the desires of her flesh. With man after man, she tried to quench her thirst, but without success! It was there, at the edge of that well, that she found the good shepherd approaching her, offering the living waters!

Unfortunately, many people do not have the Lord as their shepherd so they do not hear his voice protecting them from danger. They are dragged away by the same waters that should quench their thirst. Like the Samaritan woman, they are trying to satisfy their thirst in pleasures, work, possessions, glory, fame, or power, but they are never happy! Millions of people are thirsty for love, attention, and recognition. In the path of their lives, they look for waters that promise quick results and immediate pleasures.

Maybe today you have some thirst in your soul. What are your deepest longings? Staring at turbulent waters that the world offers will not help. Wait for the good shepherd to quench your thirst. Go after his living water because Jesus is the only one that can satisfy your longings, needs, and desires. Read what scripture says.

> Take delight in the LORD, and he will give you the desires of your heart. (Psalm 37:4)

The shepherd cares about your needs whatever they may be: financial, emotional, physical, or spiritual. When we seek him and learn to wait for him, hearing his voice and following him, we start drinking his living water!

In the next chapter, we will continue meditating on this psalm, but today I want to give you an invitation. How about putting on a paper all your thirst, fears, and anxieties that exist in your heart? Could you think about this before you write? Meditate about yourself for some moments! Then you can ask the Lord to remove all fears, anxieties, longings, and worries from you. Surrender your thirst to the Lord, for he can take care of you! He will reveal himself as the one who takes care of every detail of your life! Take time to confess to the Lord, aloud, every point written. Remember the Lord is taking you calmly to quiet waters!

> List longings, fears, and anxieties.

_____

_____

_____

_____

Day 12

PASSING THROUGH THE VALLEY

> Even though I walk through the darkest valley, I will fear no evil, for you are with me; your rod and your staff, they comfort me.
>
> —Psalm 23:4

David trusts his shepherd so much that he is willing to cross dangerous and dark places with him. With Christ at our side, there is no threat that can destroy us. David knew this in practice because he faced many situations that bordered on despair. In his youth, King Saul had tried to kill him several times! He was persecuted for years and had to hide in deserted places and caves. Perhaps someone might think that God was not with David because he was suffering such afflictions. But it was exactly the opposite! After this time of trials, David was raised as the king of Israel, honored above all.

In the task of leading sheep to quiet waters and green pastures, the shepherd often needs to lead his flock through dark and dangerous valleys. Many times, it is necessary to cross the valley of suffering, the shadow of death. These are places where light is scarce, cold and fear are everywhere, the dangers come closer, and we have the impression that we are alone. The shepherd is at our side, but the darkness of the place prevents us from seeing him well so we often despair. The despair is the result of our blindness and our wrong impressions, not by the true situation!

Maybe you have been through moments like this where despair, fear, and anguish are crushing you. Sadness invades and you find yourself overwhelmed by depression. The only thing you can see is your pain and the dangers around you. You do not feel God. You even think he has abandoned you or that maybe he is punishing you! In these moments, we need to remember with faith that he is always with us. David declared, "For you are with me."

As 2 Corinthians 7:9–11 teaches us, God uses the sorrow and the trials in life to bring maturity into our lives. In times of suffering, we need to remember the truths we talked about in chapter 10, remembering that God is not a false god or a false concept of God that we may have. He is not a "god" who takes pleasure seeing us make mistakes so he can punish us for them.

The Bible shows us that in moments of pain, your Heavenly Father is there, right beside you, crossing the same valley with you. When we are surprised by the darkest valleys, we need to trust the voice of the good shepherd who guides and leads us securely along his safe path. We can see this in Job's story. In the moment when he was suffering and in despair, Job did not know where God was, but God knew very well where Job was! Job's suffering blinded him, but not God. At the end of Job's story, he met personally with the Creator and received double everything he had lost.

When we are walking the valley, our faith is proved. There we don't see very clearly the shepherd at our side. There we can be distracted by the dangers that surround us. But the Word of God says,

> Faith is confidence in what we hope for and assurance
> about what we do not see (Hebrews 11:1).

It is exactly when we do not see, feel, and hear that we are required to continue walking. Faith is needed exactly when we don't see or feel anything! In these moments, we must ask ourselves this: what did the good shepherd tell us to do? Remember his words and obey! Faith is not feeling; it is obeying! Keep walking!

I remember when one day I broke the right window of my car.

For some days, I put a piece of black plastic to protect from the rain, before taking the car to be fixed. When I was driving it, my friend sitting to my right could see behind the plastic and tell me whether any car was coming or not. I needed to trust him! Every time I had to cross a big avenue or street, I looked at him. Every time he said, "You can go," I had to trust him and move the car, even if inside I was afraid that maybe another car was coming. But I trusted my friend so I could move! And you, do you trust in God?

On one occasion, Jesus and his disciples were crossing the Sea of Galilee by boat. Jesus had commanded them to cross, so he went to sleep. A storm started so fast that the disciples were desperate, awakening Jesus. The Lord calmed the storm and called the disciples' attention. "Why are you so afraid? Do you still have no faith?" (Mark 4:40). They should not have been afraid! After all, Jesus gave them a command: cross the lake! If Jesus said so, then no problem could stop them, not even a threat to their lives! Even though Jesus was sleeping in the boat, silent and apparently indifferent to the storm that was passing, the word they needed to hear was given in the beginning. The disciples only needed to remember and obey!

Have ever you passed through a dark valley? Perhaps you are now going through a storm that you believe can destroy you. We need to trust in the good shepherd, remembering his words and knowing that he is not a punitive "god"!

It is true that pain and suffering are often used by God to make us grow. We don't understand why we lose people, suffer from illness, and go through crises. Suffering was not God's plan for his creation but was caused by the sins of humanity. However, even though suffering and evil are the result of sin, fruits of Satan's works, God can turn curse into blessing! Read what James wrote.

> Consider it pure joy, my brothers and sisters, whenever you face trials of many kinds, because you know that the testing of your faith produces perseverance. Let perseverance finish its work so that you may be mature and complete, not lacking anything (James 1:2–4)

But David also wrote, "Your rod and your staff, they comfort me." The staff was used both to defend his sheep from wild animals and to pull them back if they were walking in wrong directions. The curved shape of the staff allowed the sheep to be hooked and brought close. We can be comforted and encouraged by the fact that our holy shepherd possesses all the power to face any external adversaries and to save us from any difficulties we may face. He even protects us from ourselves! Sometimes we are prevented from pursuing certain projects, not because we are attacked by any enemy but because God is pulling us back to himself, sheltering us from a wrong direction. If we are stubborn, fighting against the staff of God, then he uses his rod. It represents the discipline of the Lord! Knowing the dangers around or ahead, God disciplines us with his rod, sometimes taking something from us, bringing some crisis, or allowing some difficulties. The rod of God comes upon us precisely because he loves us. The Word of God is clear about this.

> Endure hardship as discipline; God is treating you as
> his children. For what children are not disciplined by
> their father? (Hebrews 12:7)

So walking the valleys of life is an experience of faith. We can pass confidently, attentive to the voice of the good shepherd, comforted by his staff and his rod. This is why Jesus, the good shepherd, gave his life for his sheep. Because of his love for us, he fought against sin and death and won! Therefore, he can guarantee to us the following:

> I have told you these things, so that in me you may
> have peace. In this world you will have trouble. But
> take heart! I have overcome the world. (John 16:33)

Jesus conquered the world, and with him, we can conquer it too! Actually, we are sent to the world to conquer it back from the hands of evil (Matthew 28:19–21), but this is a subject for another chapter! One day we will even overcome death (Luke 20:35–26; 1 Corinthians

5:25–26)! The greatest of our enemies will be conquered, and every son and daughter of God one day will rise to live eternally with our Lord. This is why we have no reason to be afraid, for even the worst of the possibilities, death, was solved by Jesus! Why should we be afraid? Meditate a few minutes on the extraordinary statement of Paul, who also described himself as a sheep guided by the shepherd.

> Who shall separate us from the love of Christ? Shall trouble or hardship or persecution or famine or nakedness or danger or sword? As it is written: "For your sake we face death all day long; we are considered as sheep to be slaughtered." No, in all these things we are more than conquerors through him who loved us. For I am convinced that neither death nor life, neither angels nor demons, neither the present nor the future, nor any powers, neither height nor depth, nor anything else in all creation, will be able to separate us from the love of God that is in Christ Jesus our Lord. (Romans 8:35–39)

I invite you to pray the following:

Lord Jesus Christ, I declare that you are my shepherd. I am your sheep. Take care of me, Lord! Help me to pass through the valleys of my life. I give you my sorrows and my tears, my challenges, and my pains. I choose to trust you, to rest in your guidance, because I know you are calmly leading me to quiet waters and green pastures. Thank you, Lord. Amen!

Day 13

FREEING THE OPPRESSED

Time flies in big cities. We usually tell ourselves that at the end of each working day. We wake up, drink coffee or tea, lose about an hour in traffic to work, sit in front of a table or desk, or spend the day on the street selling a product that promises to change someone's life. Then, when our energies have been squeezed to the last drop, we go to college, or postgraduation school, or maybe a specialization course, because we tell ourselves that to survive in this competitive world, we must always be updated. When the evening is over, we return to our home and dedicate a few moments to our family, if they are not yet sleeping. It seems that our body has arrived home but our mind is still at work thinking about what it will need to solve on the following day. We have problems with sleep. Sometimes we crash into bed, overwhelmed by tiredness, but in general, we suffer from insomnia because the problems of the day do not want to leave us. We think while we dream. We dream that we are working. When Friday arrives, our boss asks us to help him catch up on Saturday tasks or to help him with a new project on an expected holiday, and because we don't want to say no to a possible income raise or a promotion, our rest is again postponed.

Do you have trouble saying no? We always say no with our silence! We are always saying no to someone when we choose to say yes to someone else. When we say yes to a boss, sometimes it means no to our family, or to our own health, or to God. If we don't learn

73

to say no to the right things, we will keep saying no to the wrong things, usually those we should love and care about.

This is the story of millions of people who daily give their life for their work and the picture of many religious leaders who end up falling into the trap of ministerial activism. They cannot say no to pressures and find themselves dominated by responsibilities that exceed their human capability. However, they never admit this because it would be weakness and they don't want to look weak. They are trapped in a vicious cycle that brings some benefits but also destruction. This is not a virtuous call to work but a new type of slavery that is consuming many people around the world.

To work is indeed virtuous, as the apostle Paul told the Thessalonians.

> Yet we urge you, brothers and sisters, to do so more and more, and to make it your ambition to lead a quiet life: You should mind your own business and work with your hands, just as we told you, so that your daily life may win the respect of outsiders and so that you will not be dependent on anybody. (1 Thessalonians 4:10–12)

Therefore, work is important! Notice that the apostle is saying that our ambition should be to have a "quiet life"! The problem is that for many, the work becomes an idol! Maybe because the person worships money, wanting to be wealthy, or because he desires recognition. They are enslaved by this false god! Look what the apostle Paul wrote about the love of money.

> Those who want to get rich fall into temptation and a trap and into many foolish and harmful desires that plunge people into ruin and destruction. For the love of money is a root of all kinds of evil. Some people, eager for money, have wandered from the faith and pierced themselves with many griefs. But you, man

of God, flee from all this, and pursue righteousness, godliness, faith, love, endurance and gentleness. (1 Timothy 6:9–11)

The truth is that for many, they are not living a "quiet life," as the apostle Paul wrote. Like a pagan god to whom people bowed, expecting promises of money, recognition, or desirable wages, people daily serve at the altars of their work. They sacrifice their health, family, and the best moments of their lives at the altar of this idol. King Solomon made a very interesting analogy about work.

All streams flow into the sea, yet the sea is never full. To the place the streams come from, there they return again. (Ecclesiastes 1:7)

Think about these words! Just as the sea is never full, which means it is never satiated, your work, your boss, your demands will never be full. There will always be more to demand from you! Knowing the human longing for more, God put in his law a commandment that clashes with the obstinate and uncontrollable lifestyle we have. He said,

Remember the Sabbath day by keeping it holy. Six days you shall labor and do all your work, but the seventh day is a sabbath to the LORD your God. On it you shall not do any work, neither you, nor your son or daughter, nor your male or female servant, nor your animals, nor any foreigner residing in your towns. For in six days the LORD made the heavens and the earth, the sea, and all that is in them, but he rested on the seventh day. Therefore the LORD blessed the Sabbath day and made it holy. (Exodus 20:8–11)

Saturday was a day created for our rest. It means we need to interrupt our work and enjoy what the Lord gave. The meaning of the word *Sabbath* comes from the Hebrew *Shabbat,* which literally means "to cease," "to rest." When we neglect the principle of Shabbat, we sin against God, our family, and our own soul!

> What good is it for someone to gain the whole world,
> yet forfeit their soul? (Mark 8:36)

If we can't rest at least once a week, it is because deep down we don't trust the Lord and his provision. When we don't stop everything to rest, our souls become enfolded by activism, and with time, we lose the pleasure for things. Even the family can become a burden when we don't rest. The food has no taste because we just swallow it. The landscape that crosses our paths in our daily life is no longer contemplated because we don't appreciate nature anymore. Our friendships become superficial. We ourselves become frivolous. Without realizing, we become robots, slaves of other slaves. These people usually do what God never asked them to do and don't do what God entrusted them to do!

The day of rest is an invitation to delight in the creation that has been presented to us. It is when we enjoy the blessings that God gave to us. Not in a legalistic way like the Pharisees did in Jesus's time, for Jesus taught us the following:

> The Sabbath was made for man, not man for the
> Sabbath. (Mark 2:27)

In other words, the purpose of Sabbath is to set man free, not to imprison him. But Saturday is more than one day of the week. It is a principle to be followed. Rest is a lifestyle where we are invited to enjoy the Lord. We are called to delight in his nature and to love our families intensely. As Adam and Eve were placed in the Garden of Eden to cultivate it and to enjoy its fruits, we are called to cultivate our family and enjoy this precious Garden of Eden given to us.

In the book of Deuteronomy, the Sabbath is related to the deliverance provided by God to the people of Israel, taking them out of Egypt (Deuteronomy 5:15). Perhaps, like those who were under Pharaoh's oppression, you too are oppressed by someone. Maybe for you to rest one day of the week, investing time with the family is something very difficult to do. Maybe because this means financial loss or abandoning dreams. What is hardest for you to let go of will reveal the idol of your heart! Maybe the person who oppresses you is your boss so you need to decide and boldly set limits to him. Perhaps your oppressor is yourself, imposing high outcomes on yourself, assuming a burden you should not have. Or maybe your oppressor is really your passion for money or social status and you need to give up a salary or a reputation.

How is your home? How is your heart? Today is the day to make important decisions that will affect your family. Have you been controlled by greed? Renounce now the spirit of greed in the name of Jesus and decide before Christ to work for a "quiet life," to rest weekly and enjoy your family. Is your oppressor a hidden desire that always seeks to satisfy others? Renounce today the power that people exercise over you. Pray, entrusting the management of your decisions only to Christ. Don't allow other people to manipulate you, submitting again your life to their desires. Decide to submit only to God! Consecrate to the Lord every aspect of your work and day. Transform what you do into an expression of worship to the holy God.

> Whatever you do, work at it with all your heart,
> as working for the Lord, not for human masters.
> (Colossians 3:23)

> Take delight in the LORD, and he will give you the
> desires of your heart. (Psalm 37:4)

When God created the world, after each day, he looked and declared that "it was good" (Genesis 1:10, 12, 18, 21, 25, 31). It was delightful for him to see his work. When Jesus was baptized, God's voice was heard saying that he was pleased for his Son's life! What

about you? Would God say that your life is good? Can he say that your life pleases him?

Give a score for each area of your life. Try to evaluate the level of God's satisfaction in each area. Be honest with yourself. From 0 to 10, what grade do you give?

family relationship	
marriage (if married)	
work	
personal rest	
devotional life	
personal health	

Day 14

A HEART THAT DEMANDS

How is your heart? Do you have difficulties forgiving someone? Pride affects our ability to forgive. People who betrayed us, abandoned us, or hurt us are often repudiated in our hearts. Even thinking about them can bring poison to our hearts. We blame them, demanding that their moral debt to us should be paid somehow. Some debts are even unpayable from our perspectives!

The way we require the debt to be paid varies from person to person. Some "kill" their offenders in their hearts, ignoring their presence and living as if they no longer exist. However, we must remember that this murder, which happens within us, far from any human witnesses, does not go unnoticed by the Lord. He sees all! Unfortunately, we tend to think that public sins are worse than the hidden ones. Nevertheless, do not forget that our honor does not depend on people's opinion but on what the Lord thinks about us!

Some people explicitly despise what their offenders do or say, using every opportunity to mistreat, offend, and speak harsh words of hatred and irony toward them. They speak even when they are not present, demoralizing their offenders at every opportunity. By doing this, they are assuming the position of a judge without really bringing their problems to the highest judge, God. Some people go to the extreme of satisfying their desires for revenge when they physically hurt or even kill. The world has innumerable examples of people doing this every day! The Word of God is clear on this matter.

You shall not murder. (Exodus 20:13)

> You have heard that it was said to the people long ago,
> "You shall not murder, and anyone who murders will
> be subject to judgment." But I tell you that anyone
> who is angry with a brother or sister will be subject
> to judgment. Again, anyone who says to a brother or
> sister, "Raca," is answerable to the court. And anyone
> who says, "You fool!" will be in danger of the fire of
> hell. (Matthew 5:21–22)

In this second text, Jesus is clear that even if you verbally offend someone, you are already guilty of murder because in your heart you killed someone. Although we feel we have the right to speak and do what we want in order to punish our offenders, Jesus states that we run the risk of going to hell because of it! After all, if we hear that person who offended or hurt you, he or she will also blame others who hurt him or her. The cycle of sin and violence goes back to Adam and Eve if we start pointing the finger at each other. People are guilty of their violence against us, but we are also sinners who offend and have offended many others! The level of corruption of the heart is different, but we are all corrupted by sin!

Hurt people keep the offense and the offender alive within themselves, continually reliving what happened in the past. This is the idea behind remorse, when the pain is relived as a poison that never disappears. They become prisoners of their pain, drinking the poison of bitterness.

The cure for this disease comes from two important biblical principles. First, we need to understand that this is pride, which is idolatry! We need to remove the desire for revenge from the throne of our hearts. As we are not righteous, because we also killed people in our hearts, we are not good judges and need to abandon the desire to judge those who offended us. It is necessary to trust the judgment in the hands of the only one who is capable of judging with wisdom and impartiality. See what the Bible says about this.

Do not judge, or you too will be judged. For in the same way you judge others, you will be judged, and with the measure you use, it will be measured to you. Why do you look at the speck of sawdust in your brother's eye and pay no attention to the plank in your own eye? How can you say to your brother, "Let me take the speck out of your eye," when all the time there is a plank in your own eye? You hypocrite, first take the plank out of your own eye, and then you will see clearly to remove the speck from your brother's eye. (Matthew 7:1–5)

You, therefore, have no excuse, you who pass judgment on someone else, for at whatever point you judge another, you are condemning yourself, because you who pass judgment do the same things. Now we know that God's judgment against those who do such things is based on truth. So when you, a mere human being, pass judgment on them and yet do the same things, do you think you will escape God's judgment? Or do you show contempt for the riches of his kindness, forbearance and patience, not realizing that God's kindness is intended to lead you to repentance? But because of your stubbornness and your unrepentant heart, you are storing up wrath against yourself for the day of God's wrath, when his righteous judgment will be revealed. (Romans 2:1–5)

So you need to surrender to God your right to judge. Do this with faith! Present your burden; surrender it through prayer at Christ's feet. Give up this poison that is killing you! Don't expect to feel good about the offender to start praying for this. Don't do it for your opponent but for God!

In this first principle, we need to understand that we are not called to be hypocrites. When we are in audience with the divine judge, we need to pour out all our pain, suffering, and even hate regarding our offender. Many imprecatory psalms were written for this purpose, where all indignation is presented with fury before the Lord. There are psalmists who ask the Lord to totally consume their enemies, killing them (Psalm 59:13), another who asks the Lord to break their teeth (Psalm 58:6), and even one who asks the Lord to burn their enemies (Psalm 140:10). Can you imagine what these enemies did to deserve this kind of imprecatory prayer? However, the psalmists are not resorting to personal justice, just presenting their wrath to God! We must confess our anger and pain to God, trusting his judgment, not our personal righteousness. However, once we have thrown our wrath in front of God's court, we need to trust in his judgment, leaving the wrath there and never revisiting it again!

James 1:20 warns us that "human anger does not produce the righteousness that God desires." We need to trust in divine justice, offering the offender into the hand of God. Therefore, the second important principle is forgiveness! Forgiveness means that the debt has been given to the great judge and he will now deal with it.

Jesus is emphatic about our need to forgive those who have offended us. The Lord spoke about this several times. However, to forgive does not mean to forget. Many people think that they can't forgive because they can't forget what was done. But forgiving means declaring that the offender no longer owes you any debt. It also means deciding no longer to demand that the offender pays for what was done in the past. The guilt or the shame that the offender brought to you should be presented and left with Jesus. You have no right to revenge, to retrieve your honor by force. You may think that revenge may return your honor in the eyes of your family and community, but it in fact will bring great shame to you before God! Only God can judge correctly and recover our honor! The apostle Paul calls us to be wronged, instead of causing disputes with each other.

> The very fact that you have lawsuits among you means you have been completely defeated already. Why

not rather be wronged? Why not rather be cheated? Instead, you yourselves cheat and do wrong, and you do this to your brothers and sisters. (1 Corinthians 6:7–8)

We may feel wronged by the idea of forgiving someone who never asked us for forgiveness, but this is exactly what we must do to free ourselves from anger and bitterness, to walk by faith in God's righteousness. We are invited to practice unconditional forgiveness toward others, just as God forgave us unconditionally. See what the Word of God says about forgiveness.

Then Peter came to Jesus and asked, "Lord, how many times shall I forgive my brother or sister who sins against me? Up to seven times?" Jesus answered, "I tell you, not seven times, but seventy-seven times." (Matthew 18:21–22)

And when you stand praying, if you hold anything against anyone, forgive them, so that your Father in heaven may forgive you your sins. (Mark 11:25)

Bear with each other and forgive one another if any of you has a grievance against someone. Forgive as the Lord forgave you. (Colossians 3:13)

Our forgiveness should not be limited, just as the Lord's forgiveness is not limited for us. If we were aware of the number of times that we sinned and insulted God and the weight of these offenses, knowing that he forgave all freely through Jesus Christ, then we would be deeply ashamed for not forgiving those who offended us.

We must trust in the one who is the true judge, leaving in his hands our pains, emotional debts, shame, and wrath, trusting in his perfect mercy and justice! Decide to forgive because forgiveness is a decision, not a feeling. Let Jesus work in your heart, transforming your decision into deliverance and deliverance into freedom and peace of mind.

It is only after forgiving through faith that our feelings and thoughts can be changed by him, transforming us from the inside out! Open the door of this room of pains, allowing Jesus to turn on the light, open the window, and cleanse the rottenest feelings that are decomposing and infecting the rest of your life. Let him purify everything!

Many times after forgiving our offenders, we are again confronted with that familiar feeling of anguish and anger trying to become bitter again. But in these moments, we remember the decision we made to forgive; we remember that the problem is no longer in our hands but in Christ's. Remember when you forgive by faith, you are opening the door for Christ to enter and cleanse your soul, thoughts, and emotions! But cleansing takes time. Let Jesus purify everything carefully. Do not close the door!

I remember a lady I assisted a few years ago. She experienced emotional and physical pain throughout her body because of remorse. It is interesting how afflictions of the soul can directly affect our body. That lady suffered different pains in her arms and hands, but the doctors found nothing wrong with her body. Psychology calls these diseases psychosomatic, that is, having emotional causes. Through counseling, I discovered that she had not been talking to her father for more than ten years. Her father had betrayed her mother and abandoned them both. Her feelings of anger, injustice, and abandonment were so strong that she was being consumed by them, like a fire burning inside. I asked her to expose all her sorrows, and amid tears and sobs, I heard words of deep hatred and rancor.

Confessing everything was a big step for her as she had not realized that she was keeping inside her so much hate for her father. Then I ministered to her the need for forgiveness, even if he did not deserve it. She was reluctant at first but then agreed to make this decision by faith. She cried while praying, exposing her father's faults to God in a flow of tears, forgiving him for everything. The next week, she came to say that her heart was so light that she had decided to call her father.

In front of me she called him, and the silence of ten years was broken! The conversation was short and objective because she called on him to participate in the next counseling session with me. The other week he came, sat on a chair, and looked silently at his daughter who was already sitting there with several sheets of paper in her hand. I explained to him that this was a very important moment and that the intention was not to expose him but to allow what God was doing through his daughter's life. She began to read the faults and sins that her father had committed against her and her mother, saying that she forgave him with all her heart. With each new item came a new forgiveness. From the beginning, from the first time she said, "I forgive him," he started to cry. I saw the tears rolling down his face. At the end of that big list, she looked at him in tears and said, "I forgive you, Father. I love you. I miss you so much!" In tears and hiccups (including me), father and daughter embraced for several minutes, feeling the touch of God in their lives. The cross of Jesus was healing the broken relationship between them!

This is an amazing truth. When we pour our hate and anguish on Jesus's cross, relationships are healed. Because on that cross, Jesus provided the bridge between human beings and God, the road back to the Garden! But he also provided the road back to our loved ones. Jesus is the only mediator between God and humans (1 Timothy 2:5), but also between humans and humans! Read and meditate on the following verses:

> Therefore, since we have been justified through faith, we have peace with God through our Lord Jesus Christ. (Romans 5:1)

> Blessed are the peacemakers, for they will be called children of God. (Matthew 5:9)

> Bear with each other and forgive one another if any of you has a grievance against someone. Forgive as the Lord forgave you. And over all these virtues put on love, which binds them all together in perfect unity. Let the peace of Christ rule in your hearts, since as members of one body you were called to peace. And be thankful. (Colossians 3:13–15)

And you, do you need to forgive someone? Maybe several people who hurt, betrayed, or abandoned you? Do you need to forgive any violence done to you? Maybe it was physical violence, sexual abuse, or even verbal offenses? Today you can be delivered of this poison you continually drink when you remember these offenses! How about doing like the lady of the story I just described above? Make a list of the sins that have been committed against you, declaring them out loud before God in prayer. Then by faith, forgive each person by delivering them into the hands of the Lord, trusting and resting in him!

Name of the person to forgive	Offense to forgive

Prayer.

Dear Heavenly Father, I forgive _____ for doing _____ to me. I declare before you that he/she is no longer indebted to me. I deliver this offense into your hands once and for all because I trust in you. In Jesus's name, amen!

Day 15

HEALING FOR REJECTION

Unaware of its effects, a person may have their entire life shaped by the emotional experience of rejection. Rejection may lead people to develop low self-esteem with a distorted self-perception. It is the fruit of attacks of Satan with the intention of making you believe that your life has little or no value. A person who suffers from rejection becomes a servant of inward emotions, giving extreme value to what other people think. The road of rejection usually takes people to a crossroads with the choice of whether to close in on themselves, living under the oppression of false beliefs while confined by self-pity, or externalizing this suffering by rejecting others, projecting on themselves false self-beliefs in the form of anger. In both cases, the person is influenced by demonic lies, enslaved by rejection.

Examples of these lies also happen through socioeconomic conditions when we believe we were born inferior to those in a better economic situation. Also, when we suffer some type of racism, when people tell us we are inferior because of the color of our skin or because of our tribe or nationality. It is as if the world is telling us who we are, based on some aspect of our life.

To understand how rejection works in our life, I want to invite you to study the story of some important biblical characters. First, let's look at the life of Jephthah. Read what the Bible says about him.

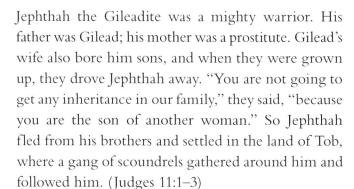

Jephthah the Gileadite was a mighty warrior. His father was Gilead; his mother was a prostitute. Gilead's wife also bore him sons, and when they were grown up, they drove Jephthah away. "You are not going to get any inheritance in our family," they said, "because you are the son of another woman." So Jephthah fled from his brothers and settled in the land of Tob, where a gang of scoundrels gathered around him and followed him. (Judges 11:1–3)

Jephthah's story began in dire circumstances. The Bible says he was a mighty warrior, but he was the son of a prostitute! There was a *but* in Jephthah's life that affected his history. His father, Gilead, had had an adulterous affair with a prostitute, resulting in Jephthah's birth. Can you realize that he was not a desired child, either by his mother or his father? For the mother, the baby disrupted her work. For the father, Jephthah was the public exposure of his shame. Every time Gilead or any one of his family looked at Jephthah, they remembered that one day when Gilead committed adultery. Jephthah was not responsible for his father's sin, but he became the symbol of sin for everyone.

As Jephthah had a *but* in his life, do you have something similar in yours? Do you have any reason to be ashamed or afraid of, which is the reason why you were rejected by someone or a group? Maybe your parents abandoned you, or your wife/husband? Perhaps it was your tribe? Do you reject yourself because of something that brings guilt and shame?

From his mother's womb, Jephthah experienced rejection. A baby desired and loved is one thing, but an unexpected child, by a woman without a husband, who would bring more difficulties to her life, is quite another This baby was not loved by either the mother or the father. Some researchers have discovered that the fetus not only shares nutrients with the mother's body but also emotions. A loved baby feels the love of its parents or its rejection! There are reports of children still in the womb so rejected by their parents that they are born and die a few days later, even though they show no physical problem. Before Jephthah was even born, he already experienced the feeling of rejection.

After Jephthah was born, he was also rejected by his family. He grew up among his half brothers and sisters who never considered him a legitimate brother. Although he was not to blame for the sins of his father or mother, people always saw him as Gilead's personified sin. His family's rejection gradually generated in Jephthah's heart the idea that perhaps they were right!

As Eve believed the serpent's lies, Jephthah started to believe Satan's lies about himself. Satan convinced Eve to eat the forbidden fruit, and now he convinced Jephthah that he had no value. The problem of rejection is not only the suffering we receive from people but the constant anguish we subsequently inflict upon ourselves as we come to believe what they say about us. We constantly relive the same rejections of the past, oppressing ourselves with the lies we have come to believe. We allow rejection to mold our self-image and the images we have of others. We are so blinded by rejection and anguish that we can't see anything else. Consequently, bitterness leads us to hatred, which may give permission to the devil. See what the apostle Paul says about this.

> In your anger do not sin: Do not let the sun go down
> while you are still angry, and do not give the devil a
> foothold. (Ephesians 4:26–27)

It is possible to be angry and not sin. However, when we do not control it but renew it the next day, and again the following day, and so on, we give place to the devil. The apostle Paul is warning us that when we surrender to hatred, whether self-hatred or toward other people, we are surrendering to demons. Consequently, the importance of forgiveness and trust in God's justice is crucial in order to be delivered from the effects of rejection because rejection produces this poison that we daily drink, dying inside. Forgiveness is the way out of rejection, not as indifference to what happened but as an act of trust in God's justice.

We forgive not because people deserve our forgiveness but mainly because we also do not deserve God's forgiveness. As sinners, we deserve death. Primarily because we also rejected God, the one who created us to be our Father. By sinning, we abandoned our Heavenly Father to live independently. We turned our backs on him. The parable of the prodigal son is our story (Luke 15:11–32)! Therefore, God was the first one to experience rejection; however, he never stopped loving us! Read what the Bible says about God being rejected.

> They sacrificed to false gods, which are not God— gods they had not known, gods that recently appeared, gods your ancestors did not fear. You deserted the Rock, who fathered you; you forgot the God who gave you birth. (Deuteronomy 32:17–18)

> But like a woman unfaithful to her husband, so you, Israel, have been unfaithful to me, declares the Lord. (Jeremiah 3:20)

> He (Jesus) was despised and rejected by mankind, a man of suffering, and familiar with pain. Like one from whom people hide their faces he was despised, and we held him in low esteem. (Isaiah 53:3)

Now read about God's attitude toward us.

> But God demonstrates his own love for us in this: While we were still sinners, Christ died for us. (Romans 5:8)

God offers us forgiveness even before we repent, inviting us to forgive others as he forgave us. When we forgive those who rejected and hurt us, we are rebelling against the diabolical cycle of rejection-bitterness-rejection in which we are trapped.

It is true that everyone experiences some degree of rejection in life; after all, we are in a world immersed in evil and full of sinners. However, there are levels of rejection that can almost destroy us, shaping our identity like the case of Jephthah. Have you also experienced a devastating type of rejection?

The climax of Jephthah's rejection was when his family expelled him from home. They didn't want to share their inheritance with him. Jephthah was so devastated that he went to live in a desert place called Tobe. The choice of that place reveals how he was feeling. Only a desert, with no life, surrounded by rocks and dust, could express his inner feelings. As he was rejected, he also rejected himself. Besides, as he was treated as a person with no value, he started to associate with other people rejected by society. He joined a group of evildoers. Why did he decide to live in a desert place? Why did he join the evildoers?

When we hear repeatedly that we are useless, cursed, inferior, and despised, we start to believe it. This is how Satan works, using people and circumstances to tell us who he claims we are. It is he who speaks to us through the people who hurt and reject us. He tells us we are worthless and we should never have been born. Little by little, we start repeating the same words in our minds to ourselves. "I'm worthless. I should never have been born. I should die." The Bible says that Satan "comes only to steal and kill and destroy," but Jesus "has come that you may have life, and have it to the full" (John 10:10). Today I invite you to hear a different voice, the voice of Jesus. He has life for you!

Jephthah sought to live in a place that reflected what he felt, accepting the judgment made by his family, inflicting upon himself the burden of living among evildoers in a desert place. Jephthah believed he was an evildoer so he joined them and became their leader! These outcasts and possibly criminals followed Jephthah not only because they saw in him leadership but because they were also rejected and marginalized as he was. Perhaps those evildoers were like Jephthah, rejected by their families or by society and trying to build their own type of family.

We must agree that modern society has generated many "Jephthahs" everywhere. Men and women rejected by their families, religious systems, and the world. People experienced in suffering and abandonment. Individuals violated verbally and physically, hurt by sexual abuse, oppressed in countless ways by Satan who has crushed them with lies. That is why Jesus came into the world, so that the truth could be proclaimed. Read what Jesus spoke about himself.

> The Spirit of the Lord is on me, because he has anointed me to proclaim good news to the poor. He has sent me to proclaim freedom for the prisoners and recovery of sight for the blind, to set the oppressed free, to proclaim the year of the Lord's favor. (Luke 4:18–19)

Are you living a miserable life? Are you a prisoner of bitterness, shame, guilt, or anger? Are you blind because of rejection? Have you been oppressed by others, maybe your family or yourself? Jesus's words are for you! He is here to set you free!

One day the Midianites oppressed the region where Jephthah's family lived, and the family had no solution to escape their oppression. So they went to Jephthah asking for help. As he became a leader, with many people following him, he was the most suitable person to lead an army in battle. However, Jephthah was hurt. How could they call him now if they were the ones who had previously rejected him?

To solve his bitterness and deep anger, Jephthah went to a city called Mispa, a place where people worshiped God. In that place, Jephthah "repeated his words before God" and accepted the request for forgiveness and the challenge of leading the army against the Midianites. When the Bible says that he "repeated his words," it means that Jephthah opened his heart before the Lord. He poured out his soul in his presence. His feelings of sadness and bitterness were "repeated," but now in front of God, the only one who could deliver and cure him.

Thus, Jephthah led the army and expelled the Midianites. Can you perceive that God used every aspect of Jephthah's life to prepare him for this moment? God was not responsible for Jephthah's sufferings, but he used the rejections and sufferings to shape him, preparing him to become the strong leader he needed to be for his people. After Jephthah "repeated his words," probably crying and expressing his anger before God because of his family, the Lord healed and changed him. God also used him mightily, bringing deliverance for the whole nation of Israel. God had a plan for Jephthah, and he also has a plan for you!

Read what the scripture says about those who are rejected.

> Though my father and mother forsake me, the LORD will receive me. (Psalm 27:10)

> God chose the lowly things of this world and the despised things—and the things that are not—to nullify the things that are, so that no one may boast before him. (1 Corinthians 1:28–29)

Today I invite you to go to your Mispa, the place where you will *repeat your words* before God. Maybe it is your room or another private place. I invite you to spend some time confessing to God everything that has hurt you since you were a child. Open your heart and expose your rejections, anger, and all bitterness you have. Reveal everything to God, hiding nothing! In that place, you can cry at the feet of the one who loves you. Spend as much time as you need. But in the end, trust in Jesus, hear his voice, and learn to rest.

> The LORD is close to the brokenhearted and saves those who are crushed in spirit. (Psalm 34:18)

Day 16

SLAVES AND PRINCES

Perhaps few people have suffered the kind of rejection that Joseph suffered when he was sold into slavery by his own brothers. His story is found in Genesis 37–47, and it is one of the most beautiful stories in the Bible, teaching us about rejection, forgiveness, and God's caring nature!

It all began when God allowed Joseph to dream when he was seventeen years old. When he told his dreams to his ten elder brothers, they were all angry at him. It turned out that Jacob, his father, had ten children with wives he did not love, while Joseph and Benjamin, the youngest, were sons of Raquel, the woman he really loved. So Jacob loved Joseph and Benjamin more than the other children.

Joseph's dreams implied that his brothers and father would one day bow down before him. Now you can understand why his brothers were even angrier. Consequently, one day they decided to kill him. That was the day that Joseph went to visit them in the field, as they were shepherds. They took him and sold him as a slave to a group of Ishmaelites who were passing by, traveling to Egypt. Consequently, Joseph went to Egypt. His brothers made up a lie to his father saying that Joseph had been killed by wild animals.

Can you imagine how Joseph was feeling? Betrayed and sold by his own brothers? Perhaps at that moment, traveling as a slave to Egypt, he asked God about that dream. "Was it a mistake, Lord?"

I can imagine him praying. "Why me?" But the answer to that question would come many years later!

In Egypt, Joseph was bought by a man named Potiphar. Joseph worked in his house and was blessed by God. Little by little, Potiphar realized that he was a good man and soon appointed him as a butler in his house. Potiphar's wife saw that Joseph was handsome and began to tempt him to have relations with her. But Joseph rejected her because he would never do that to his master, much less commit a sin against God. One day when he arrived at Potiphar's house, it was empty. Potiphar's wife was alone there, so she grabbed Joseph, trying to get him into bed. He ran away, leaving his clothes in her hands. She, in anger, called the servants, saying that it was he who had tried to force himself on her. Consequently, Joseph was arrested and sent to prison because of that woman. An injustice was inflicted on him one more time!

Rejected by the brothers, and now wronged by Potiphar's wife, Joseph's life seemed to go from bad to worse. Sometimes, in difficult times, we ask ourselves, "Where is God? Did he abandon me?" But Joseph neither criticized God nor grumbled. He trusted in his protection.

As he gave his best efforts in Potiphar's house, he did the same in prison. After some time, he became a respected inmate gaining the favor of the jailer and everyone in prison. There Joseph met Pharaoh's cupbearer and his baker, thrown into prison for some reason. One night the two had different dreams, and after telling what they had dreamed, Joseph interpreted them. In three days, Pharaoh would call the cupbearer back to work and have the baker killed. Three days later, everything happened as Joseph had said. However, the cupbearer forgot about Joseph, who stayed in prison for two more years.

How long would it take God to restore Joseph's freedom? Maybe you have asked this about yourself too. "How long, Lord?" "Why?" But we need to learn to wait on him. Trust in him, because when our lives are in his hands, even the sufferings, prison, and betrayal we experience are used by him to shape us. Nevertheless, we should not wait inactively but do our best wherever we are. As Joseph did his best in Potiphar's house, and in prison, we need to do our best in every situation God brings to us.

One day Pharaoh had a dream, and nobody could interpret it. The cupbearer remembered Joseph and his experience in prison, speaking about him to Pharaoh. So he called for Joseph, changed his clothes, and shaved him to be taken before the king. After hearing Pharaoh's dreams, Joseph interpreted them correctly, bringing great joy to Pharaoh's heart.

Seven years of plentiful food were to begin, and after that, seven years of famine would come. Pharaoh decided to put Joseph as governor over all Egypt. Only Pharaoh was above him in authority. Therefore, Joseph went from slave to prisoner and from prisoner to governor of Egypt! What a path! Could you imagine a political career starting as a slave?

The path along which God takes us to walk can sometimes be tortuous, difficult, and painful. But when we trust in the Lord, we know that in the end, it will result in life and blessing for us and everyone around us. Even if God leads us into challenging circumstances as Joseph experienced, he does not let us be destroyed. For God treats us like a goldsmith who refines gold. Like the goldsmith, God takes us to the fire to purify us, to remove our impurities, and without taking his eyes off us, he takes us to the limit. Sometimes the heat is so intense that we think that God has abandoned us. But it is in these moments that the Lord's eyes are most focused on us!

After seven years of plenty, the years of hunger began. With this, Joseph's family also began to suffer. They heard about the food in Egypt so Jacob sent his ten sons to the city. When Joseph saw his brothers, they did not recognize him, but he recognized them. They all bowed in front of him in reverence since he was the governor. Joseph then remembered his dream.

Joseph's heart was hurt. He even started to take revenge on them. He accused his brothers of being spies looking for reasons to invade Egypt. He knew they were not spies, but he was angry. He arrested and put one of them in jail, sending the others back home to bring the youngest, Benjamin, to prove who they really were. That was not necessary, but Joseph's wounded heart led him to do it.

His brothers took a long time to return because they thought he would arrest them along with the youngest. But as their hunger was getting stronger, they decided to go. When they arrived back in Egypt, Joseph called them to eat at his house. There he saw again his younger brother, Benjamin, and went to a separate room to cry.

Have you ever done something wrong, maybe motivated by revenge, and immediately realized that it was a mistake? We have no right to take revenge because when we carry out justice with our own hands, we become as guilty as the person on whom we are taking revenge, if not more so. If Joseph had continued to act motivated by rejection and anger, he would have done the same thing his brothers had done, becoming as wrong as they were. And then, who would avenge them on Joseph? Think about it. Revenge always begets revenge. Only a servant of God who trusts in divine justice and mercy can break this cycle by submitting to the Lord.

Joseph developed a strategy of revenge. When his brothers were coming back home with their bags, he asked someone to put a silver cup in Benjamin's bag. After his accusing them of theft, and finding the cup, they were desperate. Judah, his brother, asked Joseph to let Benjamin go, offering himself to be his slave in Benjamin's place. Now think about this carefully!

Judah was not guilty of Benjamin's sin, but he offered himself to pay the price of his brother's fault. One day, the great-grandson of Judah, Jesus Christ, effectively did this for us. Jesus, as the elder brother, God's incarnation as a human being, offered to die on a cross because that was our destiny! As Judah, Jesus declared that we should be let go, to be free, because he would pay for our sins! When we give our life to Jesus, we can be sure that we are delivered of our guilt, set free of Satan's power, cleansed of our shame!

Joseph could not contain himself and ordered his servants to go away, leaving only him and his brothers. Joseph could not accomplish his plan of revenge, repenting, and crying. He cried loudly and declared that he was Joseph, their brother, stating that they should not be saddened. His weeping was so loud that even in Pharaoh's house it was heard. At that moment, Joseph said something to them that is one of the most precious lessons of this whole story.

> And now, do not be distressed and do not be angry with yourselves for selling me here, because it was to save lives that God sent me ahead of you. For two years now there has been famine in the land, and for the next five years, there will be no plowing and reaping. But God sent me ahead of you to preserve for you a remnant on earth and to save your lives by a great deliverance. So then, it was not you who sent me here, but God. He made me a father to Pharaoh, lord of his entire household and ruler of all Egypt. (Genesis 45:5–8)

Joseph declared that God was in control of everything. God allowed Joseph to be sold into slavery so that he could protect his family from great hunger. Joseph realized God's sovereignty and his care in every detail. He forgave his brothers, knowing that God had used his wounds and pain precisely to promote their salvation. The apostle Paul also speaks about this principle.

> And we know that in all things God works for the good of those who love him, who have been called according to his purpose. (Romans 8:28)

If we know that God acts in all things, we can rest in him. We don't need to take revenge. We can trust and rest in him because he knows everything and uses even the sins of others to promote his good intentions.

We believe that the family is a project of God. However, because of human sin, it is through the family that much of our traumas, rejections, and sorrows settle in our hearts. Cursed words thrown at us hurt immensely. Abandonment and betrayal sometimes have the power to crush us entirely. Nevertheless, we need to follow Joseph's example in forgiveness. As we discussed previously, even after our conversion we sometimes carry idols in our hearts, which can even be our family! Breaking the cycle of rejection–rage–rejection toward our relatives leads us to a relationship of love and maturity with God and his church.

So can you recognize God's purposes in your own life story? Perhaps not yet. But don't be discouraged because God loves us, and he is in control of everything. Today I invite you to meditate on this story applying it to your life. You may identify yourself with the slave Joseph rejected by his brothers. Maybe with the wronged Joseph or the prisoner. It is important to remember that whatever Joseph's situation, he honored God with all his heart. Even when he started down a road of revenge, he repented and changed his way. What about you? How about changing today the road along which you are walking and following God's direction?

Day 17

LEARNING TO SEE

After Adam and Eve sinned, they realized they were naked. They were already naked before eating the fruit, but scripture says that they felt no shame (Genesis 2:25). Have you ever thought about why suddenly they realized that they were naked? In reality, they felt shame, anger, and fear inwardly, as a result of their sin. However, they had never felt that before. Now they tried to understand that feeling, projecting it into nakedness. They wrongly interpreted that the problem was their nakedness. They began to see their reality with distorted eyes, treating what was once sacred as something shameful. Sin twisted their gaze, making them project upon nakedness the shame and guilt that was inside their hearts.

Sin always distorts the way we see ourselves, others, and every situation in life! Like looking through a glass, sin conditions us to interpret life wrongly. We think that our problem is something or someone when many times we are the ones responsible. We simply cannot see reality because our spiritual eyes became blurred. Adam put the blame for his sin on Eve when in fact he was to blame. Eve blamed the serpent when she herself desired to sin. How easily we find someone to punish for our mistakes.

Without realizing it, we do the same as Adam and Eve. We look for something physical to take the blame for what is spiritual. This is how culture was created, as compensation for Adam and Eve's sin. We do not see within our hearts the desperate fear dominating us.

We misinterpret people, intentions, and facts and choose wrongly. We project onto others the wrath we feel toward our own sin and think that they are the reason for all our misfortunes.

A terrible experience of sexual abuse can produce the misunderstanding that you are homosexual. The abandonment of a father has the same power, producing a longing for fatherhood that is misunderstood as a desire for men. The attraction to the same sex usually hides a deeper desire for an absent father or a neglectful mother. What is behind your desires? What is the shame behind your nakedness? What is the fear behind your fear? What is the real problem that makes you see everything distorted?

The apostle Paul wrote,

> The wrath of God is being revealed from heaven against all the godlessness and wickedness of people, who suppress the truth by their wickedness. (Romans 1:18)

Our distorted lens leads us to "suppress" God's truth. We don't want to admit our faults so we create excuses for ourselves and others. We become godless and wicked people. Inwardly we know we are wrong, but we project our faults upon others. God's truth is inwardly present within us in the form of our fear, shame, anger, and different types of anxieties. We suffer when we suppress his truth, diving into a life of wickedness. Read what the apostle Paul also wrote.

> Furthermore, just as they did not think it worthwhile to retain the knowledge of God, so God gave them over to a depraved mind, so that they do what ought not to be done. They have become filled with every kind of wickedness, evil, greed and depravity. They are full of envy, murder, strife, deceit and malice. They are gossips, slanderers, God-haters, insolent, arrogant and boastful; they invent ways of doing evil; they disobey their parents; they have no understanding, no fidelity, no love, no mercy. Although they know

God's righteous decree that those who do such things deserve death, they not only continue to do these very things but also approve of those who practice them. (Romans 1:28–32)

I don't want to offend you, and this was not Paul's intention. Paul's words were written to open our eyes to perceive that our sins are the result of our depraved mind, which has retained the knowledge of God and suppressed his truth. However, today is the day that God wants to open your eyes, making you see!

After feeling ashamed, Adam and Eve made clothes. They tried to hide something spiritual with the fig leaves. We do the same, trying to hide and avoid our own shame, guilt, and anger. We produce different types of "fig leaves" for each feeling! For example, when we are faced with shame for being caught in some mistake or failure, our tendency is not to confess the sin but to create a story that fakes our sin. The story is a fig leaf hiding our shameful act. Besides, because of shame, we try to build a social image in order to get a reputation of honor in front of people.

As declared before, human attempts to stop the pain of fear, anger, guilt, or shame only produce illusions of protection. It is like building transparent walls around our house so that people who pass by on the street do not see what is really happening. Low self-esteem, narcissism, homosexuality, pride, and so many other illusions created by us are nothing more than fig leaves that hide nothing, and only camouflage. Deep down we must deal with our shame every day, even if we don't know for sure what it is. We must keep our eyes open, abandon the illusions the devil leads us to believe, and deal with this truth. But we don't need to deal with it alone. Jesus invites us to deal with each one of our fig leaves, approaching him in repentance, renouncing each one of them, and with faith, because Jesus wants to open our eyes and heal our shame.

One day a lady came to me asking for help. She confessed that she had problems with men, claiming that no relationships ever worked because every man was always a bad person. She started relationships and discarded each one of them. As I began to hear from her, asking about her life, she told me what happened when, as a little girl, she was sexually abused by her grandfather. As a child, without properly understanding what had happened, she developed a sexual compulsion throwing her into the arms of different boys. She discarded them after seducing them. After narrating her life story, she started to understand why she was doing the same thing after many years. I asked her if she hated her grandfather, and she said yes. She realized that she was dominated by anger toward her grandfather, and while she was enslaved by pleasure, she was also enslaved by a repulsion for men. Because every man was a representation of her grandfather!

When she understood that she was stuck in a vicious cycle, avenging her abuse upon those men, her eyes were opened. When she realized her sin, she forgave her grandfather herself and asked Christ to allow her to see men as he saw them. She was brave to expose her shame to me and to God, so God cured her, forgave her sins, and gave her a new identity as a daughter of God. From a shameful condition to an honorable one! She decided to stay alone for a while. About a year later, she met a man of God. They fell in love with each other and later got married. Today, after many years, she ministers to other women who are stuck in the same blindness that she was!

That girl was wounded by Satan through her grandfather. The wound distorted her vision of men and pleasure. It was only after allowing Jesus to touch her spiritual eyes that she started to see herself and everything clearly. Jesus said,

> Then you will know the truth, and the truth will set you free. (John 8:32)

Knowing the truth is more than merely recognizing it. It means experiencing the truth. It is more about knowing, like tasting the flavor of a certain fruit rather than just being aware of its existence. Jesus is not only bringing awareness of your blindness but is inviting you to allow him to touch your spiritual eyes. Jesus also said,

I am the way, and the truth, and the life; no one comes to the Father except through me. (John 14:6)

Truth is only perceived through Jesus Christ. He needs to be our "glasses" to correctly see life, others, ourselves, and everything. When we start to see through him, we realize that we believed many lies about ourselves and others. We said previously that Jesus is the only mediator between God and man (1 Timothy 2:5–6), but he is also the mediator between us and others and must be the mediator between us and ourselves. This means that when we see ourselves, we need to use Christ as the proper lens, as our Redeemer and Savior, as our goal of existence. Therefore, we need to forgive ourselves because Jesus already died for our sins. It also means that we need to see our parents, friends, and even our enemies with Jesus in the middle. Forgiveness becomes our lifestyle. Jesus is the only one who can shape our eyes to see through his love and mercy!

One day Cain and Abel, the first sons of Adam and Eve, decided to offer a sacrifice to God (Genesis 4). Abel offered the best of his flock, while Cain did not offer sacrificially. God was pleased with Abel's offering but not with Cain's. Cain looked at the situation with a distorted gaze, thinking that he was rejected by God because of Abel, when in fact it was only his offering that was rejected. God himself told him,

> Then the LORD said to Cain, Why are you angry? Why is your face downcast? If you do what is right, will you not be accepted? But if you do not do what is right, sin is crouching at your door; it desires to have you, but you must rule over it. (Genesis 4:6–7)

Cain was not looking at the situation correctly. He did not see the evil trying to dominate his heart. Instead of recognizing that he did not offer his best to God, he looked at his brother as being responsible. Cain was blinded by his anger, feeling wrongly rejected by God, so he decided to put an end to the one who in his mind had stolen the acceptance of the Lord. What a wrong interpretation! Consequently, Cain killed his brother.

This is what sin does. It leads us to hurt those whom we should love, to treat as enemies those who are our allies. We look at the beautiful world and see it ugly and treat the ugly as beautiful. We take the good as evil and the evil as good. We need humility to admit that our eyes are blurred. Our perception is distorted. The way you see people is probably not right! This is what the apostle Paul is saying here.

> To the pure, all things are pure, but to those who are corrupted and do not believe, nothing is pure. In fact, both their minds and consciences are corrupted. (Titus 1:15)

Today I invite you to write a list of the main events of your life. From your birth until today, what are the main moments that have marked you? Good and bad events, sins committed against you, and by you. After you do this, pray a prayer similar to this one:

> Dear Lord, you are powerful and loving, I recognize that I am blind. I admit that my view of myself and my problems is distorted and wrong. I admit that my judgments are all flawed and I need help. I need a cure for my blindness. Please give me vision and discernment. Show me the lies I have believed. I ask you in the name of Jesus Christ. Amen.

After writing down the sins committed by you and against you, and praying, write next to the event the lies you started to believe because of that episode. Maybe not all of them led you to believe lies, so don't worry about writing an explanation for all of them. But spend some time meditating on your own life in the light of the scriptures, seeking to remember what false truths you have assimilated or learned or behaviors you have come to practice because of these unique events. Write them side by side. At the end, on a separate sheet, write down the decisions you need to make based on what God revealed to you about yourself. Pray for these decisions and allow Christ to free you from the lies you have believed. Obey what he tells you to do! I know this is a big assignment I am asking you to do. But it will be a great blessing to you if you really dedicate some time to doing it! God bless you!

Day 18

DO NOT BE AFRAID

Fear is one of those emotions that every human being who lives and those who have lived before have already experienced. Every man and woman experienced it, and those who are still to be born will certainly experience it. Fear is part of our fallen nature. For some people, fear is an easy feeling to overcome; for others, it is an almost impossible task. Today we will see how Christ frees us from fear.

Fear paralyzes. It anesthetizes our reason and can lead us to do what we would never do. For many, fear is a controlling power whereby everything in their lives is governed by its demands. When we allow fear to sit on the throne of our heart, we become its submissive vassals. We carry their flag wherever we walk. We are always under its servitude.

Being afraid involves expecting the worst. Fearful eyes usually see misfortune in every corner of life. Sometimes people are afflicted by past events, fearing that they will repeat them in their lives, so they surrender to fear. They live thinking about the probability of a new suffering, a new disappointment, a new sorrow. They raise walls around themselves to protect themselves from possible suffering—walls based on the illusion of false safety. They surround themselves with excuses for not relating deeply to people for fear of being hurt by them. They isolate themselves so much that they end up also being blocked from other people's love. They are hostages to their fear of rejection.

Those seized by fear have serious problems with self-esteem. It is as if a black lens obscures their eyes. They have difficulty dreaming about the future because fear is a negative belief. It always believes in the worst. Therefore, fear must be seen as a form of doubt.

If we are controlled by fear, it is because we do not trust in God. We want to control all the circumstances around us, to have dominion over everything offering risk. But this is idolatry! Fear has become a type of idol ruling over us!

I have already experienced a deep fear. I was close to dying a few times in my life. None of them, however, was the fruit of my irresponsibility. Always the result of events that were totally out of my control. One of these moments was when I was in Nepal during the earthquake that devastated that nation in 2015. For several days, we experienced tremors when houses, buildings, and light pylons fell like sheets of paper. I was there to help the victims in the villages present in the mountains. But how to go there if the tremors were rolling giant stones from the top of the mountains? The force of nature was so strong that a river even changed its course. Buildings were collapsing, making many victims.

I remember at a certain moment sitting in the middle of a dusty street, putting my hands on my head. I was desolated by the real possibility of dying. The smell of dead corpses and some terrible images got stuck in my mind. The tremors happened unexpectedly, and by the time we realized it, something had already collapsed. *Will I be the next victim?* I thought. What control did I have over my life? Certainly none! I felt completely powerless. That day I made a video recording a message to my wife and daughter, sending it to a friend so that she would send it in the case of my death. The situation created a scenario that made me allow fear to control me. After all, people were screaming and running for their lives every time a tremor happened.

At a certain point, in the middle of that dusty street, God spoke to me. The Lord reminded me that he was the one who brought me there, telling me I had no reason to fear. He was in control of everything! Instead of looking at the deaths and dangers, the Lord made me look at him! God brought to my mind several verses that I knew by heart but had forgotten. He reminded me of Psalm 91. At that moment, I took my eyes off the dust of that road and turned them to the blue sky above my head, reciting mentally,

> Whoever dwells in the shelter of the Most High will rest in the shadow of the Almighty. I will say of the Lord, He is my refuge and my fortress, my God, in whom I trust. (Psalm 91:1–2)

God reminded me that my task was to live in his shelter, in the intimacy of his presence, that he held me calmly in his arms, for he was my fortress. When we seek God's will, we come to live in his secret place and no longer need to be afraid. The heavens may thunder and the earth tremble, but who can take us from the arms of the Almighty? As the apostle Paul wrote, "If God is for us, who will be against us?" (Romans 8:31). On that afternoon in Nepal, the Lord reminded me of his promise of protection and rest.

> Surely he will save you from the fowler's snare and from the deadly pestilence. He will cover you with his feathers, and under his wings you will find refuge; his faithfulness will be your shield and rampart. You will not fear the terror of night, nor the arrow that flies by day, nor the pestilence that stalks in the darkness, nor the plague that destroys at midday. A thousand may fall at your side, ten thousand at your right hand, but it will not come near you. (Psalm 91:3–7)

I was literally watching it happen. Nothing was hitting me. I had a mission and I needed to accomplish it! I challenged people to climb the mountains and serve the victims of the earthquake. God gave me an unshakeable faith that affected other brothers who were with me. We understood that if God sent us, then he would protect us. And that is what happened!

The problem is not to be afraid but to surrender to it. We can trust in the protection and care of the Lord. If we look back, we will see what God has done in the lives of his servants. He protected Joseph in the midst of countless adversities. He helped the whole nation of Israel by opening the Red Sea so that they could pass through it and stay dry. He fed thousands of people with manna, bread that literally fell daily from the sky. The Lord gave victory to Gideon with only three hundred soldiers facing an army of thousands. He made the teenager David conquer the fearsome giant Goliath. This God who made the walls of Jericho collapse can also make the walls of your fear come down! If giants and nations have succumbed before him, what can he do more for you? Just trust in Christ, walk in his Spirit, and learn to rest in his power. Meditate on what the Lord has said to his servants and today is speaking to you.

> Do not be afraid of them; the LORD your God himself
> will fight for you. (Deuteronomy 3:22)

> Be strong and very courageous. Be careful to obey all
> the law my servant Moses gave you; do not turn from
> it to the right or to the left, that you may be successful
> wherever you go. (Joshua 1:7)

> Then you will have success if you are careful to
> observe the decrees and laws that the LORD gave
> Moses for Israel. Be strong and courageous. Do not
> be afraid or discouraged. (1 Chronicles 22:13)

> "Do not be afraid of them, for I am with you and will
> rescue you," declares the LORD. (Jeremiah 1:8)

> And you, son of man, do not be afraid of them or their
> words. Do not be afraid, though briers and thorns are

all around you and you live among scorpions. Do not be afraid of what they say or be terrified by them, though they are a rebellious people. (Ezekiel 2:6)

List of fears.

_____

_____

_____

_____

_____

Prayer.

Heavenly Father, I give my fear of _____ before you today. I decide to trust you, Lord, with all my heart! I will no longer be controlled by it in Jesus's name. Amen!"

Day 19

CUTTING THE THORNS

Jesus tells us a very interesting parable about a sower who sowed his seeds in different soils. This parable is in Matthew 13:1–9. The Lord tells us that a portion of the seeds fell in the middle of the way, another among the stones, another among thorns, and finally, some fell on good soil. Jesus explains that the seed is the Word of God, and the soil is the human heart. Each heart responds differently to God's Word, but only those who have "good soil" germinate the Word, growing and producing fruits. What is the soil of your heart?

I want to call your attention to the soil that is full of thorns. Jesus declared that the seed germinated and sprouted but gradually was suffocated by the thorns, slowly causing the plant to die. There are many thorns that can suffocate us. Some are the reasons we are afflicted by anxiety, fear, and depression. These thorns oppress us so much that they take away the joy of living. Jesus said that the thorns are the "worries of this life and the deceitfulness of wealth" (Matthew 13:22). Which thorns are suffocating you? Today I want to meditate about some of the thorns that people allow to grow in the gardens of their lives in this modern age.

The first thorn is entertainment, which is everywhere in our daily life. Entertainment is not sinful in itself but today has become a type of idol dominating every aspect of life. We are living the age of entertainment! It is on television, in electronic games, available on our cell phones, and on the internet. More and more, we see people becoming addicted to games, to series of streaming platforms. We are addicted to instant messages, social media, funny videos, and so many things that suck our time like a vampire sucking our blood. Pornography has become one of the greatest disasters of our time, breaking up marriages and corrupting youths and teens. It has become a devastating drug available to anyone anywhere, just a few clicks away. The thorns of entertainment have suffocated many people, and it is no wonder that we see an increase in people suffering from anxiety and depression.

We are so used to watching videos, movies, and series that we have stopped perceiving many immoral values behind the stories. If we spend time watching immoral, violent content, often with scenes that take time to rid our minds of, we are allowing spiritual garbage to be deposited in our hearts.

Our thoughts will be full of images and desires similar to what we have seen. These thorns can suffocate the Word of God within us! What do you think you will reap from your life if you sow in your heart scenes of violence, death, sensuality, and betrayal? Think for a moment. Do your thoughts and feelings reflect the type of entertainment you are stuck with? Who knows if your aversion to sex or pleasure is the result of filling your mind with erotic films and videos? Perhaps your impatience, violent words, and aggressiveness are the result of watching or playing content filled with these.

If we waste too much time with entertainment, we become sick. Try eating only chocolate or ice cream for a week to see what happens to your health. The same happens with entertainment. Excessive entertainment harms our souls as sugar affects our bodies! Compare the time you spend on entertainment with the time you dedicate to God in prayer and his word. Compare the time you spend on social media, or a cell phone, with the time you spend with your family! How can you cut these thorns that are suffocating your life?

I am not giving you a legalistic orientation, telling you to stop watching TV and end all the entertainment in your life! What I am saying is that you need to cut out every entertainment that is controlling your life. If you don't have self-control, it is better to cut it. If something is not glorifying God, then it needs to be cut. We need to discern the type of movies we watch or the games we play. Would you watch this movie with Jesus sitting with you? We need to control the time we spend on social media or any other entertainment.

Another thorn is too much interest in the life of others. Just as the world is overly entertained by movies, each one of us can spend too much time trying to "watch" the life of people we know. It can be either a relative who lives next door or someone from a distant place. Some people focus their energy on watching people's lives, trying to discover how their marriage is, the children's education, family income, and many other issues. This type of curiosity is often based on sinful motivations, also leading to sinful outcomes. People busy with the lives of others usually fall into the sin of backbiting, slander, insult, and envy.

Sometimes, because your eyes are so focused on others, you end up neglecting what you have, ignoring the precious blessings given by God. Consequently, people fall into deceitful frustration. That's why men start desiring their neighbor's wives and women start desiring the husbands of other women. The neighbors' house looks better than ours, as well as their possessions, their money, their everything. People covet everything in their minds, amusing themselves with other people's lives in sinful ways. What about turning your eyes away from other people's lives and looking at your own?

When the serpent started the conversation with Eve, he captured her attention to look at the forbidden fruit. The serpent's lie sowed frustration in the heart of Eve, who thought about the only thing she was not allowed to possess. Eve turned her eyes away from the rich and delightful Garden given by God, staring at the only thing she was forbidden to eat. Are you also distracted looking at the forbidden fruits in the world, forgetting the Garden that God already gave to you?

Another thorn is senseless activism. This is a lifestyle involving an accelerated rhythm, always busy focusing on productivity. The desire to enrich overshadows the eyes, burdens life, and sucks out our spiritual vitality. Little by little, the Word of God fades within us. Many people say they don't want to be rich, but the truth is that they can't admit this desire they have. Their self-esteem depends on what they have. Spiritual blindness does not allow them to see how obsessed they are by status, possessions, and power. They feel important when they are always busy and guilty when are resting. This is why they can't invest much time in prayer and Bible study, because in their minds this is a waste of time. Read what the great preacher A. W. Tozer wrote about this.

> No shortcut exists. God has not bowed to our nervous haste nor embraced the methods of our machine age. It is well that we accept the hard truth now: The man who would know God must give time to Him. He must count no time wasted which is spent in the cultivation of His acquaintance. He must give himself to meditation and prayer hours on end. So did the saints of old, the glorious company of the apostles, the goodly fellowship of the prophets and the believing members of the holy church in all generations. (From the book *God's Pursuit of Man*).

In their impulse to be the best or to experience the best, people become slaves to money. They become suffocated by the constant obligation to work more in order to reach or maintain a specific lifestyle. Read what Paul wrote.

> Having what to eat and what to wear, let us be satisfied with it. (1 Timothy 6:8)

> Those who want to get rich fall into temptation and a trap and into many foolish and harmful desires that plunge people into ruin and destruction. For the love of money is a root of all kinds of evil. Some people, eager for money, have wandered from the faith and

pierced themselves with many griefs. (1 Timothy 6:9–10)

Cutting the thorns may mean living a simpler but healthier life. Cutting expenses, spending more time with family and with God. I met a family that every year "needed" to do an expensive trip with their children. They were proud to tell this to their friends and liked to post their children's photos on social media. However, the father of that family was consumed by work. When he was finishing paying for one trip, he was already in debt for another. He was tormented with the obligation to always have a new car. His life was empty, and so was his relationship with his wife. They were clearly not happy, but on social media, people thought they were the happiest family in the city! His children only saw their father on weekends because he always arrived home late. One day he couldn't take it anymore. He suffered a crisis in his marriage that led him to review everything. He was getting money but losing his wife and children. He was able to purchase the most expensive toys, but all his children wanted was their father.

He chose to live a simple life, and everything changed! Slowly he worked less, focusing only on what was essential and necessary. Their marriage flourished, and the children experienced their father's love with intensity.

Have you been suffocated by thorns like these? A common excuse we receive from people invited to a prayer meeting is "I don't have time" or "My day is short because I am too busy." With these excuses, we prove to God that we are being consumed by thorns, serving idols. We even go to church, but if the service takes much time, we get impatient and complain that the preacher spoke too long. We value our time on television, the internet, leisure, and the cell phone much more than our time with God.

The more connected we are to the virtual world, the more disconnected we become from the real world. People today are alienated from real affections. May we wake up from our sleep and cut every thorn suffocating us. Less internet and more family. Fewer games and more real interactions. Fewer movies and more Bible. Less cell phone and more bent knees in prayer. Less social media and more real fellowship with the church!

If we do not control our time, activities, and entertainment, these thorns will daily grow in the garden of our hearts. Eventually, we will be suffocated and spiritually die!

Below write a list of activities that are consuming your time. What usually occupies your mind? What are the thorns suffocating you?

Write.

_____

_____

_____

_____

_____

Now ask God in prayer to deliver you from each item written. Surrender each one before the throne of God. By faith cut them out of your life, asking for God's grace! The Holy Spirit will enable you to cut them. What decisions do you need to take today?

Day 20

THE SIN AGAINST THE BODY

God did not create man to live alone. Genesis 2:18 says that the Creator decided to make the woman a "helper suitable to him." Within God's perfect plan was the complementarity of genders. Man and woman are complete with each other, not only physically but also emotionally and psychologically. Sexuality was created by God with a purpose, and it has a place: marriage!

> That is why a man leaves his father and mother and is united to his wife, and they become one flesh. (Genesis 2:24)

This is a sacred union created by God! However, Satan also distorted what was made to be a blessing, turning it into a curse. Fornication, prostitution, adultery, immorality, pornography, and homosexuality are some of the countless distortions related to sexuality. For those who practice these things, sexual pleasure has become the idol sitting on the throne of their hearts. Let's read what the Bible says about it.

> It is God's will that you should be sanctified: that you should avoid sexual immorality; that each of you should learn to control your own body, in a way that is holy and honorable, not in passionate lust like the

pagans, who do not know God. (1 Thessalonians 4:3–5)

This text is clear about God's will: to abstain from sexual immorality. Immorality means any sexual practices outside marriage. If you are not married but involved sexually with another person, this is sexual immorality. If you regularly access pornography, this is also sexual immorality. If you are married but seek sexual pleasure with another woman or man, then you are committing adultery. Read what King Solomon wrote about the holiness and blessing of marriage.

> Drink water from your own cistern, running water from your own well. Should your springs overflow in the streets, your streams of water in the public squares? Let them be yours alone, never to be shared with strangers. May your fountain be blessed, and may you rejoice in the wife of your youth. A loving doe, a graceful deer—may her breasts satisfy you always, may you ever be intoxicated with her love. Why, my son, be intoxicated with another man's wife? Why embrace the bosom of a wayward woman? For your ways are in full view of the LORD, and he examines all your paths. The evil deeds of the wicked ensnare them; the cords of their sins hold them fast. For lack of discipline they will die, led astray by their own great folly. (Proverbs 5:15–23)

Solomon taught that a husband should drink from his own cistern and not from other sources. He makes it very clear what he is talking about, also making it clear that conjugal love is to be enjoyed between a husband and his wife! He also affirms that the wicked ones are ensnared by the cords of their sins, meaning that they become enslaved by their sexual desires. Many men and women are today addicted to sensuality, just as King Solomon described. See another text written by the apostle Paul.

> Do you not know that your bodies are members of Christ himself? Shall I then take the members of Christ and unite them with a prostitute? Never! Do you not know that he who unites himself with a prostitute is one with her in body? For it is said, "The two will become one flesh." But whoever is united with the Lord is one with him in spirit. Flee from sexual immorality. All other sins a person commits are outside the body, but whoever sins sexually, sins against their own body. Do you not know that your bodies are temples of the Holy Spirit, who is in you, whom you have received from God? You are not your own; you were bought at a price. Therefore honor God with your bodies. (1 Corinthians 6:15–20)

Our body is the temple of the Holy Spirit. We must not unite our body with a prostitute because this profanes the name of Christ in us. It destroys the holiness of the temple that is our body. It is evident that Solomon's and Paul's words aimed at men are also directed at women!

Unfortunately, many people are stuck in sexual sin, addicted to lascivious relationships that open huge doors for oppressive demons. When they come, they lead people to even worse conditions. The apostle Paul says that the wicked ones are abandoned to their sinful passions. Read what he says about this.

> Therefore God gave them over in the sinful desires of their hearts to sexual impurity for the degrading of their bodies with one another. They exchanged the truth about God for a lie, and worshiped and served created things rather than the Creator—who is forever praised. Amen. Because of this, God gave them over to shameful lusts. Even their women

exchanged natural sexual relations for unnatural ones. In the same way the men also abandoned natural relations with women and were inflamed with lust for one another. Men committed shameful acts with other men, and received in themselves the due penalty for their error. (Romans 1:24–27)

Paul clarifies that the wicked ones reach the extreme of exchanging their sexual relations, talking about lesbianism and homosexuality. A mind that is controlled by sexual desire cares only about self-satisfaction, losing shame, and forgetting his or her true identity. It is necessary to confess and abandon every sexual sin committed, repenting genuinely, renouncing before God the idol of sexual pleasure.

Jesus goes even deeper about sexual immorality. See what he said.

You have heard that it was said, "You shall not commit adultery". But I tell you that anyone who looks at a woman lustfully has already committed adultery with her in his heart. If your right eye causes you to stumble, gouge it out and throw it away. It is better for you to lose one part of your body than for your whole body to be thrown into hell. And if your right hand causes you to stumble, cut it off and throw it away. It is better for you to lose one part of your body than for your whole body to go into hell. (Matthew 5:27–30)

Jesus stated that adultery or sexual immorality occurs in the heart when we simply look lustfully at a woman (or a man). When we feed libidinous thoughts about someone of the opposite sex, we are already committing adultery in our minds. The eyes of some people are always seeking the sinful. The sin exposed by Jesus is not to desire, but the imagination of the heart! That act of self-imagining in sexual immorality is an act of adultery! Jesus is making clear that even what we conceive mentally is done before God. After all, God is not only the Lord of our material world but also the Lord of every possible world we can create in our minds. There is no escape from his presence!

We must listen to what the apostle Paul says about the thoughts we must have in our minds.

> Finally, brothers and sisters, whatever is true, whatever is noble, whatever is right, whatever is pure, whatever is lovely, whatever is admirable—if anything is excellent or praiseworthy—think about such things. (Philippians 4:8)

In other words, taking care of our thoughts is to take care of our spiritual lives. Paul is presenting a filter we must use because, if our minds are not occupied with what is true, noble, right, pure, lovely, and admirable, our hearts will be always longing for sin. We will always be seeking to quench our hidden desires somehow. This is what Paul is also saying in this text:

> So I say, walk by the Spirit, and you will not gratify the desires of the flesh. For the flesh desires what is contrary to the Spirit, and the Spirit what is contrary to the flesh. They are in conflict with each other, so that you are not to do whatever you want. (Galatians 5:16–17)

Our flesh represents our exteriority, and the Spirit our interiority, because God's Spirit now inhabits the ones born again. If you want to overcome the tyranny of your desires, the only road is to walk by the Spirit. Listen to his voice, seek his face, and obey his commands.

Jesus was even more radical about sexual immorality. He said to pluck out the eyes and hands and throw them away! Yes, I believe he meant this literally. For those who cannot control themselves, it is better to mutilate themselves instead of being thrown into hell. Many interpret this text metaphorically because they can't admit the seriousness of sexual purity for our spiritual life. What is a hand compared to eternity? By making this radical proposal, Jesus leaves no doubt regarding the seriousness of the problem.

We must also ask ourselves this: what is feeding our thoughts and leading us to sin? If it is television, we must apply Christ's command and pull it out and throw it away! If it is the internet, the movies, or perhaps a worldly friendship, we must not hesitate; cut and throw it away! Sanctify your eyes, your mind, and your body, surrendering to the Lord everything that is corrupting you! Read the following verses and meditate about what you are going to do when you finish reading this chapter!

> Put to death, therefore, whatever belongs to your earthly nature: sexual immorality, impurity, lust, evil desires and greed, which is idolatry. (Colossians 3:5)

> Therefore, I urge you, brothers and sisters, in view of God's mercy, to offer your bodies as a living sacrifice, holy and pleasing to God—this is your true and proper worship. Do not conform to the pattern of this world, but be transformed by the renewing of your mind. Then you will be able to test and approve what God's will is—his good, pleasing and perfect will. (Romans 12:1–2)

Day 21

DENY YOURSELF!

Sexual pleasure has become in our times the great idol worshipped. On television almost everything is sold with a woman or a seminude man alongside. Movies, novels, books, and magazines all insert spicy stories making our imagination travel through the universe of pleasure. Some music explicitly displays sexual dances, or has subjective lyrics, where we consume them without thinking. We are numbed by these pleasures. But as soon as the pleasure evaporates, our emptiness becomes bigger and a new dose urges within.

However, it is not only by the internet or films that our minds are anesthetized, but also by some religious rituals and teachings that worship sexual pleasure. In Islam the ambition is to go to a paradise full of virgins for the pleasure of the faithful. I once heard an imam describing the shape of the legs, bellies, and breasts of these supposed virgins in paradise! What type of paradise is this? Although sex is a taboo in Islamic culture, the fact that in many Muslim societies women need to be fully covered reflects this religious yearning for sexual pleasure, evidencing how their men can't control themselves.

Hinduism and other Asian religions use a demonic tripod to seduce and imprison people: the philosophical doctrines defining human life according to mystical teachings, the pantheism of gods shaped in the image of man's sinfulness, and sexuality as a form of worship and devotion. If the Hindu god Brahma raped his own daughter, why can't his followers do the same? The god Shiva is almost always depicted in explicit sexual positions so that even though Hindu devotees try to explain it philosophically, the truth is evident because it sexually appeals!

The pagan religiosity of many Hindus and animists regarding the cult of fertility, and other forms of sexual rites, has confined people to a vicious cycle of pleasure and pain. No wonder that rape is a big social problem in these societies, as are collective assaults whereby men violate a woman and kill her in shame. Sexuality was created by God as a blessing for the marriage between a husband and his wife, but when it is worshiped, it becomes a curse, oppressive, and deadly.

In some tribal societies, men have power over every woman in their village. Nobody belongs to anyone, and even little girls suffer abuse at a very young age, and this demonic behavior is considered normal! Some of them celebrate public sex as a ritual to the spirits. Some tribal leaders in Africa even claim the first night with a wife who gets married. Can you see how Satan corrupts people and societies through different distortions in sexuality? It is no wonder why sexual immorality is on every list of sinful and dangerous practices warned about in the New Testament. If we have been controlled by our impulses for pleasure, we must carefully listen to Jesus's words.

> Then Jesus said to his disciples, "Whoever wants to be my disciple must deny themselves and take up their cross and follow me. For whoever wants to save their life will lose it, but whoever loses their life for me will find it". (Matthew 16:24–25)

Denying yourself is perhaps the greatest challenge. Saying no to your will, desires, and self-interest is only possible if you believe that God has the best for you. Refusing to follow your fleshly longings demands climbing the Calvary following Christ. It is like Abraham climbing Moriah to sacrifice his only son (Genesis 22), believing that God's will is perfect for he has a plan for us!

In Genesis 34, we have a very sad story about how Dinah, a

daughter of Jacob, was seduced by Shechem, a prince in Canaan. The text says that Shechem spoke to her heart and possessed her. After her brothers heard what had happened, they planned an act of revenge, killing Shechem's family.

Dinah heard the boy speaking to her heart. Maybe her heart fluttered in excitement listening to him speak in her ear. Perhaps he used beautiful words with a seductive voice, just as women are attracted. However, when she was alone with him, he abused her, humiliating her before everyone. Her humiliation attracted the wrath of her brothers, who later killed Shechem and his family. How vulnerable a woman can become when she longs for love and attention and suddenly a man appears speaking to her heart. Beware. Not every man approaches with pure intentions!

Another important story is that of Amnon and Tamar, son and daughter of King David (2 Samuel 13). They were half brothers from different mothers. The Bible says that Tamar was very beautiful. Amnon was attracted to her and planned to sleep with his half sister! He did not love Tamar and had no intention of marrying her, also not caring that she was his half sister. Setting up a strategy with his friend Jonadab, Amnon pretended to be sick, asking Tamar's help to prepare something for him to eat. When Tamar entered his room with some cakes, he held her and raped her right there. She resisted him, but he was controlled by the thought of satisfying his desire. After raping her, he despised and expelled her. She was destroyed by the shame, attracting the anger of his brother Absalom. To cut a long story short, two years after this event, Absalom killed Amnon in revenge and organized a revolt against his father, David. After all, David had not disciplined Amnon. What a sad story that unfortunately is like many others today!

Amnon was controlled by his flesh and did not think about the consequences. Some men often do not think about the effects of their actions. They do not deny themselves. Men and women need to be suspicious of their flesh, never trusting the desires burning in the body. However, if you are truly in love with someone and can't control your flesh, you should listen to Paul's words.

But if they cannot control themselves, they should marry, for it is better to marry than to burn with passion. (1 Corinthians 7:9)

Perhaps you are a woman who has been used by a man and discarded like Tamar. Maybe you were not abused like her because you gave yourself up deliberately, but then you were thrown away like a rejected object in the same way. Maybe you are a man who has used and discarded women in your life. Maybe you are a parent, like David, who is ignoring the abuse happening right next to you. The disgrace of a person passively following his flesh is similar to a father passively neglecting his responsibility. The victim feels abused twice when a parent neglects his or her responsibility!

However, how can we deny ourselves? How can we control our flesh? I want to give you some practical guidelines here. First, if you are living in a sexually active relationship with someone but you are not married, you need to get married. Maybe you have crossed the limits in your relationship and nobody knows about it. Remember that you are always in front of God, so he knows everything! So end this relationship or get married! You were called to be holy, separated by God, to live a pure life as the temple of the Holy Spirit!

Sexual desire is like a fire burning in the body. Your being saved does not exempt your body from being attracted to sin, so you need to be careful not to set a fire in your house! So learn to keep your home, which is your mind and heart, always clean and renewed. Do not allow dirty and erotic thoughts to take over.

Do not conform to the pattern of this world, but be transformed by the renewing of your mind. Then you will be able to test and approve what God's will is—his good, pleasing and perfect will. (Romans 12:2)

Change your thoughts by changing the direction of your eyes. Stop looking at anything that leads you to sin. If you take care of your eyes, you will keep your focus on the right place.

> The eye is the lamp of the body. If your eyes are healthy, your whole body will be full of light. But if your eyes are unhealthy, your whole body will be full of darkness. If then the light within you is darkness, how great is that darkness! (Matthew 6:22–23)

Make an alliance with your eyes as Job did.

> I made a covenant with my eyes not to look lustfully at a young woman. (Job 31:1)

Subjugate your body like Paul.

> No, I strike a blow to my body and make it my slave so that after I have preached to others, I myself will not be disqualified for the prize. (1 Corinthians 9:27)

Pray that God will give you self-control; he can and wants to give you it! Subjugate your body, trusting in the Lord. When we read that we must deny ourselves, we imagine a life without pleasure and empty. But this is not true. True pleasure comes from Christ and his Holy Spirit. The only way of subjugating the desires of our flesh is walking in the Spirit, being satisfied in Christ. Read what the apostle Paul wrote about the acts of the flesh and the fruit of the Spirit.

> The acts of the flesh are obvious: sexual immorality, impurity and debauchery; idolatry and witchcraft; hatred, discord, jealousy, fits of rage, selfish ambition, dissensions, factions and envy; drunkenness, orgies, and the like. I warn you, as I did before, that those who live like this will not inherit the kingdom of God. But the fruit of the Spirit is love, joy, peace, forbearance, kindness, goodness, faithfulness, gentleness and self-control. Against such things there is no law. (Galatians 5:19–23)

When we learn to drink from the living water, we are no longer thirsty. We produce fruits and flourish in rejoice. When we inhabit God's presence, we find self-control. We learn to be delighted in the Lord.

> Take delight in the LORD, and he will give you the desires of your heart. (Psalm 37:4)

When we learn to trust him and deny ourselves, we begin to truly delight in his presence and to rest in him! It was God who created sexual pleasure but planned it for marriage. To marry the person you love, dedicating your body to him or her, is God's plan. It was for marriage that he designed our sexuality!

I can't conclude this chapter without saying that some people are called to be celibatarians. It is not for everyone, and it is not a command of the Lord. Those living in celibacy are not better than those married, and vice versa. Nevertheless, as declared by the apostle Paul, the celibatarian can better focus on the work of God. If you feel this is the way for your life, let the Holy Spirit confirm it in your heart.

> For there are eunuchs who were born that way, and there are eunuchs who have been made eunuchs by others—and there are those who choose to live like eunuchs for the sake of the kingdom of heaven. The one who can accept this should accept it. (Matthew 19:12)

> An unmarried man is concerned about the Lord's affairs—how he can please the Lord. But a married man is concerned about the affairs of this world—how he can please his wife—and his interests are divided. An unmarried woman or virgin is concerned about the Lord's affairs: Her aim is to be devoted to the Lord in both body and spirit. But a married

woman is concerned about the affairs of this world—how she can please her husband. I am saying this for your own good, not to restrict you, but that you may live in a right way in undivided devotion to the Lord. If anyone is worried that he might not be acting honorably toward the virgin he is engaged to, and if his passions are too strong and he feels he ought to marry, he should do as he wants. He is not sinning. They should get married. But the man who has settled the matter in his own mind, who is under no compulsion but has control over his own will, and who has made up his mind not to marry the virgin—this man also does the right thing. So then, he who marries the virgin does right, but he who does not marry her does better. (1 Corinthians 7:32–38)

Have you sinned sexually? Today you will confess each one of these sins to the Lord, asking for his forgiveness and purification! What in your life needs to be denied? Confess this to the Lord too. Make a list of your greatest struggles, and in sincerity declare them to the Lord. Ask his Holy Spirit to fill you and give you strength!

_____

_____

_____

_____

_____

_____

> Prayer.

Heavenly Father, I confess that I have not lived a pure life. Please purify and sanctify my life to glorify you. I confess that I did _____. Today I decide to rip out of my life _____ because it leads me to sin. Give me the strength to deny myself and overcome this sin! In the name of Jesus Christ I ask. Amen!

Day 22

THE PROBLEM OF THE HUMAN HEART

Adam and Eve's fall was not only the responsibility of Satan but also of Adam and Eve. They allowed into their hearts the desire to be like God! The serpent seduced our first parents with the same desire that led Satan himself to sin and lose his position as an angel of the Lord. Today this evil desire is a poison present in every human being because of sin. It infected our hearts with the same corrupted feeling of living independently, self-sufficiently. It is a virus that has contaminated everything and everyone in our life.

Jesus demonstrated that our heart is the source of attitudes, the true origin of our problems. He compared the man to trees (Matthew 7:16–19) and the words and actions to fruits produced. The fruits we produce are directly related to our hearts. Therefore, it is meaningless when a person tries to change his behavior when his heart is still unchanged. For a genuine change, we need a revolutionary transformation in the quality of our hearts! A transformation from the inside out!

As Oswald Smith wrote, "The heart of the human problem is the problem of the human heart!" It is in our hearts that we hide different idols. Through our search for earthly things, like fleshly pleasures, power, possessions, and personal glory, we allow idols to take control. They come quietly through our invitation and slowly take control of everything. These idols can blind you from seeing what is valuable and what is not. They deceive us, making us exchange our diamonds for glass stones, attracted by a matte shine.

Many idolaters never bow in front of an image but daily bend inwardly in the worship of their desires. For many, the idol is the craving for recognition, to be admired, desired. For others, it is the sensuous gratification or a yearning for power. These desires in themselves are not evil; however, when we surrender to any of them, it becomes a god governing our lives. Like an arrow, we aim our hearts in the direction of these desires, and when we release the arrow, a powerful movement dominates, controlling everything. Only the external intervention of God can change the course of our hearts!

In most of the cultures in the east, in Hindu, Muslim, and Buddhist countries, honor is highly valued. Consequently, people rate appearances more than truth. The search for respect and personal glory in the eyes of a community usually comes at the cost of truth and integrity. Lying is a very common practice in these contexts! The prestige of being admired by people is like a fig leaf trying to hide the shame. This existence in self-contradiction, of being admired and honored by people, but living in shame before oneself and God generates a life of deep anxiety and anguish. If our fancy clothes, our wearing of expensive jewelry, envious cars, and other adornments are intended to attract attention to us, then we have already fallen into the trap of vanity. Read what the apostle Peter wrote about beauty.

> Your beauty should not come from outward adornment, such as elaborate hairstyles and the wearing of gold jewelry or fine clothes. Rather, it should be that of your inner self, the unfading beauty of a gentle and quiet spirit, which is of great worth in God's sight. For this is the way the holy women of the past who put their hope in God used to adorn themselves. They submitted themselves to their own husbands. (1 Peter 3:3–5)

This word is not restricted to women as many men are also captured by vanity! Besides, Peter is not saying that we should not use beautiful clothes or that we can't buy good cars or use jewelry. What he is saying is that these things can control our lives through vanity so our real adornment must be in the spirit. We should not focus on our personal glory but on God's glory. Center our hearts not on how we appear to other people but on how we are presented before God!

As the Lord despises those who make sculptured images, he also loathes those who raise altars in their own hearts. The greatest spiritual battle is for the dominion of your heart! See what James wrote in his letter about the desires and passions in our hearts.

> What causes fights and quarrels among you? Don't they come from your desires that battle within you? You desire but do not have, so you kill. You covet but you cannot get what you want, so you quarrel and fight. You do not have because you do not ask God. (James 4:1–2)

The source of our evil deeds is in our covetous hearts. The heart is the true battlefield for our freedom! It is in the mind where Satan has entrenched himself to overpower us. On our emotions, he launched his fiercest attacks to subjugate everything. We need to conquer back every inch of our hearts by subduing every thought, feeling, desire, and belief under the lordship of Christ! Can you identify in your own heart the altars you have raised? James even calls them "adulterers" (James 4:4), because idolatry is indeed spiritual infidelity.

We must be aware that an idol does not appear in our hearts overnight. It sprouts slowly within like a weed. First, we have a desire, naive and not sinful. When we allow this desire to grow in our hearts, it becomes very important. If we do not stop its growth, it suddenly becomes a necessity! Consequently, the desire starts to make demands. When it goes from "important" to "necessary," it became an idol ruling from the inside. When this idol is not satisfied, it generates frustration, unhappiness, sadness, anger, anxiety, and eventually depression. Many suicides are motivated by idols demanding something that cannot be achieved.

As an example, let's think about an event in King David's life. David knew who God was and experienced his power and love at different moments in his life. However, he allowed his heart to be dominated by a wrong desire. David gave space to a desire for another man's wife (2 Samuel 11). He watched the beautiful Bathsheba bathing, because his palace was higher than other houses and he could see things without being noticed. Instead of avoiding looking, he allowed his desire to feed his mind.

What was he doing in that higher place? Why was he looking down at the people's houses? Why was he idle if a war was happening and he was the king? When we are idle, or when our minds are empty, we become vulnerable to Satan's attacks and the weakness of our flesh!

David hatched a diabolical plan resulting in adultery and in the murder of Bathsheba's husband, hiding his sin. Like David, many powerful people also sin and hide, using their power and influence. Power makes them believe they are above any law. However, nothing can be hidden from the eyes of the King of kings, the Supreme Judge. God confronted David, exposing his sin. The seed of David's desire grew in his heart, producing adultery and murder. God brought about hard consequences for him.

Another person who was dominated by his desire was Judas Iscariot. Scripture reveals that in Judas's heart was a wrong motivation. He wished for money. Not even walking with Jesus, seeing his miracles, hearing his messages, stopped Judas feeding his hidden desire for wealth. Notice that being part of a church, or even a leader as Judas was, you can be living hypocritically. If your motivations are not aligned with Jesus's will, your religious acts are meaningless!

In Luke 22, we observe Judas bargaining with the Jewish priests about the bribe to give false testimony so that Jesus could be arrested. Perhaps he did not imagine what was going to happen to Jesus because when he saw Jesus's imminent crucifixion, he returned to the temple and threw his coins to the ground, dominated by remorse. Judas immediately committed suicide.

The great differences between remorse and repentance are faith and tears. Repentance admits sin but believes in God's forgiveness. Remorse only sees the evil done, believing it to be unredeemable. Repentance reduces the person to tears, like Peter after denying Jesus. Remorse leads to darkness and death, as Judas after his betrayal! Repentance takes us to self-humiliation in front of God. Remorse takes us to death because the idol of our pride doesn't allow us to bow. What road are you going to choose?

Judas's desire for wealth resulted in the death of an innocent. Similarly, many times our own desires for money, fame, pleasure, recognition, power, honor, control, and affirmation do the same! We are led down paths that hurt us and the people around us. God does not want you to be a slave to idols in your heart. To get rid of these idols, you need to give up your own selfishness and decide to surrender your desires, motivations, and dreams before the Lord.

Today you can renounce your heart's desires. Destroy the idols remaining in the throne of your soul. Let the Lord show you the idols that need to be toppled. Let Jesus become the only Lord of your whole life. Read and meditate on the following verses. After doing that, write down the idols of your heart and pray a prayer similar to the one below. Stop being a vassal of these idols and bow before Jesus in total submission.

> Jesus replied, "Very truly I tell you, everyone who sins is a slave to sin. Now a slave has no permanent place in the family, but a son belongs to it forever. So if the Son sets you free, you will be free indeed." (John 8:34–36)

Idols of my heart.

_____

_____

_____

_____

_____

Prayer.

Heavenly Father, I confess that I have idols in my heart. Today I expose you that I gave space to the desire of _____. Today I dethrone the idol _____ and ask you to set me free! I will no longer serve my desire. I give the throne of my heart to you, Lord Jesus. Amen!

Day 23

DEFEATING PRIDE

Pride is the strongest idol dominating the human heart. The church father St. Augustine called it the source of all sins! Pride can appear in different expressions, such as narcissism, self-promotion, self-pity, arrogance, and always focusing on the ego. Pride was what caused Satan to fall, being cast out of his position as God's anointed cherub (Isaiah 14:13–14; Ezekiel 28:17; 1 Timothy 3:6). In fact, his pride was his desire to take God's place. This is why his temptation to Eve inseminated her mind with the same sinful desire.

Every false god in every religion expresses pride. Pay attention to the Hindu idols that are part of Indian culture, influencing millions of lives! If you know their fables, you have probably noticed how pride is a strong mark on their identity. Moreover, even though in the Hadiths of Islam pride is condemned, the life of their prophet teaches otherwise. Motivated by pride, he led twenty-seven military operations and ordered fifty more. He was responsible for the murder of thousands of people. Therefore, whether through the example of false gods or false prophets, Satan always inspires pride.

Still, unlike the Hindu writings that exalt pride through poems, stories, and doctrines, or the example of Mohamed and his followers' lives surrounded by violence, the Bible teaches the opposite! God himself came down to earth as a man, living a simple life to communicate his message. Jesus not only spoke but offered himself humbly to die in our place. Read what Paul wrote about him.

he made himself nothing by taking the very nature of
a servant, being made in human likeness. And being
found in appearance as a man, he humbled himself by
becoming obedient to death—even death on a cross!
(Philippians 2:7–8)

If God humbled himself by becoming a man, even dying on a
cross to save us, what should be our attitude? Jesus's example was the
opposite of the false gods and false prophets. Instead of crucifying
our enemies, Jesus invites us to go up to Calvary for them. Instead of
taking revenge on being offended, Christ calls us to turn the other
cheek and love our enemies (Matthew 5:38–48). Jesus does not say
that the leader should wear fancy clothes and be served by others, but
he himself set the example by taking off his own robe and washing
the feet of his disciples (John 13:1–20). Jesus said that he did not come
to be served but to serve (Matthew 20:28). Read what the Word of
God tells us about pride.

> When pride comes, then comes disgrace, but with
> humility comes wisdom. (Proverbs 11:2)

> Do nothing out of selfish ambition or vain conceit.
> Rather, in humility value others above yourselves.
> (Philippians 2:3)

> For all those who exalt themselves will be humbled,
> and those who humble themselves will be exalted.
> (Luke 14:11)

Pride is what makes us avoid true repentance. The proud ones
don't ask forgiveness. Pride is also what keeps us from forgiving
others. Pride often leads to conflict and the emergence of feelings,
such as hatred and a desire for revenge. Pride makes us fail with
people we should love. We make decisions based on our own will and
break meaningful relationships because of our inability to admit our

mistakes. So what is the solution to our pride? The prophet Jeremiah, inspired by the Holy Spirit, declared,

> This is what the LORD says: "Let not the wise boast of their wisdom or the strong boast of their strength or the rich boast of their riches, but let the one who boasts boast about this: that they have the understanding to know me, that I am the LORD, who exercises kindness, justice and righteousness on earth, for in these I delight," declares the LORD. (Jeremiah 9:23–24)

To boast, or to be proud, will be meaningless if it is based on our own strength, intelligence, or wealth. We should be proud for only one reason: knowing the Lord intimately. Unfortunately, our trust is often based on our ability, not on God's mercy and power. We are deceived by believing in Satan's lie of self-sufficiency. See what James teaches us.

> Submit yourselves, then, to God. Resist the devil, and he will flee from you. Come near to God and he will come near to you. Wash your hands, you sinners, and purify your hearts, you double-minded. Grieve, mourn and wail. Change your laughter to mourning and your joy to gloom. Humble yourselves before the Lord, and he will lift you up. (James 4:7–10)

James goes to the center of our heart's problem saying that we must submit to God and resist the devil. We need to do this starting with our own repentance before the Lord, turning our joy into crying, and admitting before the Lord our sins, failures, and errors of the present and the past.

We need to confess our inability to solve our own problems, heal our wounds, or free ourselves from evil behavior. While we try to lead our lives by our own abilities, we will not be able to find genuine peace. God's transformation begins in our complete submission and unrestricted surrender.

I was betrayed by a girl many years ago. We had a relationship and she cheated on me with another man. I remember how hurt I was and how I built a wall round myself because of that. I was expecting her to come and ask my forgiveness. But she never came, and slowly I became controlled by pride. Suddenly I stopped caring about people, only thinking about myself and how unhappy I was, how disastrous my experience had been, falling into proud self-pity. My relationship with God was affected and I felt nothing but my pain. I distanced myself from my family and could not bear the eyes of my church brothers and sisters. My pride dominated me.

Until one day God visited me in my car as I was driving downtown. He spoke to me through a song that was playing. I remember it like today. I stopped the car and started crying. I hadn't cried in a long time for my heart was hardened. I cried and asked God's forgiveness for demanding something that was not in my hands. I should not have assumed the posture of a lord, a judge, or a god! What was in my hands now was to forgive her and seek in Christ the affirmation and love that only he could give me. I needed to assume my human condition, approaching God as the Almighty, trusting in his will. In that car, God healed me. I felt like he was pulling something heavy out of me.

What about you listening to God's voice today?

Prayer.

Eternal Father, I surrender before you today. Forgive my sins, my pride, my arrogance. Without you, I am nothing. I desperately need you, Lord. I surrender into your hands the lordship of my life. Come reign over all aspects of my existence and accomplish in me what you desire. In the name of Jesus Christ, amen!

Day 24

BLESSED ARE THOSE WHO MOURN

Many people in different societies believe that crying is a sign of weakness. We are taught to be strong, and tough, even in situations of loss and suffering. We learn to sweep frustration under the carpet of our emotions. We hide in the drawers of our souls the feeling of loss, the pain of bad experiences suffered. We conceal our disappointments with others and with ourselves, hiding everything. Or at least we try!

Regarding our sins, we do the same. We know we are wrong, but our hearts do not allow us to admit it. Acknowledging that we are liars and that we have deceived ourselves and others is totally unacceptable because we learn that from our cultures. Indeed, to accept our situation as miserable sinners, selfish, and arrogant is totally countercultural. But this is the road scripture points us to!

When we read the Bible, we see in its sacred mirror our corrupted images. We realize that we are liars, idolaters, thieves, murderers, prostitutes, and adulterers. We know that we are evil and that our sins are the reason to be deeply ashamed. When we have a personal encounter with Jesus, the incarnated God, the darkness of our life is evidenced by the light of his! But if we approach him with a humble stance, believing in Jesus's love and power, his light dispels our darkness!

We are like that prodigal son who decided to abandon his father, only interested in his inheritance. He left for the world to enjoy his momentary pleasures. Like the prodigal son, we also left God's house, trying to live by ourselves. Because of this, many are taking care of pigs wanting to eat what the pigs eat. Shame takes hold of us, but we still resist repenting and returning to the Father. We can go to the Holy Father if we humble ourselves, but many prefer to stay with the pigs.

Our pride and presumption still hold us from accepting we have failed and are unable to run our lives properly. That's why we need to cry! The need to weep is urgent, removing what dams our heart before God. Going against everything the world and our cultures tell us, Jesus declared,

> Blessed are those who mourn, for they will be comforted. (Matthew 5:4)

Genuine repentance always comes with tears! Not those tears of manipulation but the sincere pouring out before God. Crying is exactly what James urges us to do.

> Come near to God and he will come near to you. Wash your hands, you sinners, and purify your hearts, you double-minded. Grieve, mourn and wail. Change your laughter to mourning and your joy to gloom. Humble yourselves before the Lord, and he will lift you up. (James 4:8–10)

David wept when he admitted his sin of adultery and murder. Peter cried when the cock crowed, and he realized his three denials of Jesus. The whole nation of Israel that returned from the Babylonian captivity cried when they heard the Word of God, perceiving that they were living in iniquity. David saw that he was an adulterer and a murderer. Peter saw he was a coward and a liar. All the people of Israel saw themselves as traitors and adulterers! Crying was the natural result of coming to terms with the sin and their degrading condition. That is why they cried. In the weeping, they evidenced repentance. This is the kind of sadness we experience when the Word of God confronts us. This is what Paul told the Corinthians.

> Yet now I am happy, not because you were made sorry, but because your sorrow led you to repentance. For you became sorrowful as God intended and so were not harmed in any way by us. (2 Corinthians 7:9)

Are you sad because of your situation? Then cry before the Lord. Break yourself before him.

> My sacrifice, O God, is a broken spirit; a broken and contrite heart you, God, will not despise. (Psalm 51:17)

Being indifferent to your sins is what the Bible calls "hardening" of the heart. Scripture alerts,

> So, as the Holy Spirit says: Today, if you hear his voice, do not harden your hearts as you did in the rebellion, during the time of testing in the wilderness. (Hebrews 3:7–8)

Jesus was once visiting a certain Pharisee when a woman known for her sins entered his house (Luke 7:36–50). She poured expensive perfume on Christ's feet. Crying the whole time, her tears fell on the Lord's feet, and she wiped them with her own hair. She did this in an attitude of deep worship and humiliation. The Pharisee looked down on the woman, but Jesus, who knew what he was thinking, told him,

> Then he turned toward the woman and said to Simon, "Do you see this woman? I came into your house. You did not give me any water for my feet, but she wet my feet with her tears and wiped them with her hair. You did not give me a kiss, but this woman, from the time I entered, has not stopped

kissing my feet. You did not put oil on my head, but she has poured perfume on my feet. Therefore, I tell you, her many sins have been forgiven—as her great love has shown. But whoever has been forgiven little loves little." Then Jesus said to her, "Your sins are forgiven." (Luke 7:44–48)

That woman was aware of her sins, so she poured herself out at Christ's feet. She did not care what the Pharisee thought. She didn't care about her reputation. She just wanted to demonstrate her love and deep gratitude to Jesus. Her attention was totally focused on him! She cried because she knew her condition as a sinner, humbling herself before Jesus. The Pharisee's heart and this woman's heart were tuned totally differently!

How long will we worry about what people think of us but neglect how Jesus sees us? How long will we hide our tears of repentance preventing Jesus from forgiving and healing us? When we cry at Jesus's feet, he heals us. As he said to that woman, he tells us the same. "Your sins are forgiven."

Today I invite you to cry! Close the door of your room and pour out your soul before Christ. Speak what you need to speak. Confess what still needs to be confessed. Like a spear piercing our hearts, we need to understand what Jesus suffered for these sins. We must open our hearts to God in the same way that an adulterous wife would confess her sins to her husband, like a son who abandoned his father and is now returning home. Cry, repent, pour out your soul, but believe that Jesus is listening and forgiving everything. When you finish, commit to change!

The LORD is close to the brokenhearted and saves those who are crushed in spirit. (Psalm 34:18)

Those who sow with tears will reap with songs of joy. Those who go out weeping, carrying seed to sow, will return with songs of joy, carrying sheaves with them. (Psalm 126:5–6)

He heals the brokenhearted and binds up their wounds. (Psalm 147:3)

He will wipe every tear from their eyes. There will be no more death or mourning or crying or pain, for the old order of things has passed away. (Revelation 21:4)

Day 25

THE POWER OF WORSHIP

We read in the first book of Samuel that King Saul disobeyed the divine order several times, so he ended up tormented by an evil spirit (1 Samuel 16:14–15). It was on this occasion that the servants summoned the teenager David, still a shepherd who played the harp in the worship of God. When he played, the evil spirit used to leave Saul. As David played, the unclean spirit withdrew from the king (1 Samuel 16:23). In this account, we have a glimpse of the power that true worship exercises over the spiritual world! It is no wonder that later David himself, who was perhaps the main poet in the Bible, wrote,

God dwells in the midst of praise (Psalm 22:3).

David experienced the powerful presence of the Lord, seeing evil spirits depart because of worship. The worship of God is powerful to free any heart from Satan's bonds. Ties of bitterness, anger, sadness, discouragement, and unbelief fade away as we approach with praise for our Heavenly Father.

If we are discouraged, lacking the will to worship him, we must by faith decide to do it otherwise. When we sacrifice our sorrows and inability to rejoice and worship him by faith, our spiritual chains are broken. It is precisely in these moments when we decide to worship God despite the circumstances that praise operates powerfully. They are sacrifices of praise!

Paul and Silas were once arrested for preaching the Gospel in a city called Philippi (Acts 16). The two were placed in a prison with their feet clamped in stocks. Paul and Silas had every reason to complain, but they didn't. They kept their hope in the Lord and began to pray and praise him. They worshiped, singing songs of praise to the Lord in that prison. Do you know what happened next?

> About midnight Paul and Silas were praying and singing hymns to God, and the other prisoners were listening to them. Suddenly there was such a violent earthquake that the foundations of the prison were shaken. At once all the prison doors flew open, and everyone's chains came loose. (Acts 16:25–26)

Similarly, there is no prison, chain, shackle, or fortress in our hearts that can resist the power of genuine worship. It is precisely in times of adversity, when we ourselves have been thrown into some dark dungeon, or when we have been imprisoned by something stronger than ourselves, that praise is most needed! By murmuring and complaining, we prevent sacrifices of praise from taking place, and we fail to experience God's power.

Once, a teenage girl, at the end of a service that I preached, manifested demons. Almost everyone had left already, so we closed the door to cast out those evil spirits. Only the leaders remained and the worship team. The girl screamed and went into contortions, cursing God with all her breath. The demons resisted and did not want to leave the girl, as she had many ties of bitterness and hatred allowing those demons to remain.

The worship team was playing a song, but they were scared. The Holy Spirit spoke to me that we needed to change the posture of our hearts. I went to the team and told them that more important than singing or playing were praising and worshiping! I asked them to forget about the girl and what was happening, putting their attention totally on God, worshipping with all their hearts. When the team began to pour themselves out before God in genuine worship, the demons began to scream in pain. The demons were suffering because of that worship! Consequently, we expelled the demons in a few seconds, for genuine praise is indeed powerful!

When we praise, we let go of our problems and connect with the One who has all the power! We move our eyes from the difficulties and turn them to the Creator. Praising is a choice of faith whereby we decide to stop seeing through our suffering and context, to see through God's eyes, who operates the impossible. By faith, we can worship the Lord when we are sad. Sincere tears are precious to the Lord (Isaiah 38:1–5; Revelation 7:17). When we pour ourselves into genuine worship, the prison of our soul is shaken by God's earthquake.

But when we keep our eyes fixed on the problems, the weight on our shoulders seems to increase, and little by little we are crushed. Have you ever felt overwhelmed by so much oppression? Satan uses our trivial problems, our unsolved feelings, our disquieting anxieties, and our hidden sins to keep us from worship. We stop reading the Bible, lose our confidence in prayer, and only complain. We murmur to ourselves, or to those around us, saying in various ways that our life is heavy. If you have really felt oppressed, then listen to Jesus.

> Come to me, all you who are weary and burdened, and I will give you rest. Take my yoke upon you and learn from me, for I am gentle and humble in heart, and you will find rest for your souls. For my yoke is easy and my burden is light. (Matthew 11:28–30)

When we break our self-sufficiency, our pride, and drop our masks before God, we surrender before him in sincere worship. If we learn to worship God every day, we can find in him rest for our souls. No demonic oppression can resist the power of Christ released in worship.

It was Jesus who showed the importance of worship, for the day before his crucifixion, at the holy supper, he and the apostles sang to the Lord (Matthew 26:30). In worship and prayer, Peter and

John cried with the church for divine intervention, when the house where they were gathered trembled (Acts 4:24–31). After suffering persecution from the Sanhedrin, they praised God for the privilege of suffering for Christ (Acts 5:41). The early church praised God with the apostles (Acts 2:47). And the apostle Paul urged the church at Ephesus not to get drunk with wine but to be filled with the Holy Spirit through song and praise (Ephesians 5:18–19). The Bible invites us to worship, to praise God with everything we are!

Today you have two invitations. The first is for you to find a private place where you can be alone with God. There, you can start asking the Lord to help you to forget worldly or pagan songs you used to sing in the past. These melodies and lyrics, instead of leading you to worship the One God, led you astray. It can be a song with a sinful appeal, a repetitive song from Islam, or some mantra that you learned and for years repeated invoking false gods. Ask the Holy Spirit to free you from false forms of worship that were part of your old nature!

After this, I invite you to start praising the Lord with all your heart. Pour out yourself in adoration as you never did before. Pray, sing, worship, cry, raise your hands, bow in submission to God. Only you and the Lord! Jesus set you free to worship him, so adore him with your whole being!

Day 26

JOINING THE BATTLE

The fact that we have a relationship with God does not liberate us from battles. In fact, it is very likely that at the beginning of our journey with Jesus, the struggles in life may even intensify. This is because we have an enemy who wants to destroy us, kill our faith, and lead us back to the slavery of sin. Satan, the great tempter, is the one who opposes us, oppressing, persecuting, and seeking to destroy us. The apostle Peter warns us about this.

> Be alert and of sober mind. Your enemy the devil prowls around like a roaring lion looking for someone to devour. Resist him, standing firm in the faith, because you know that the family of believers throughout the world is undergoing the same kind of sufferings. (1 Peter 5:8–9)

In the Old Testament, God promised the land of Canaan to the descendants of Abraham. But when they arrived to take possession of the Promised Land, centuries after Abraham died, they realized that it was occupied by very strong nations with fortified cities.

God had given it to them and now it was necessary to conquer the land. Maybe some of them thought, *If God gave it to us, why do we need to conquer it?* The promise is fulfilled not by the strength of our arms but by the Lord who answers our faith and uses his power through our obedience. God's promise is true, but we must conquer it through faith and obedience. This is because, as we mentioned in the first chapters, humanity gave the authority of this world to the serpent. Now Satan is ruling in many areas of our society, nature, and people's lives. Jesus came to reestablish God's kingdom, and he invites us to conquer back everything for God.

The apostle Paul wrote some magnificent guidelines in the book of Ephesians regarding this spiritual battle that every Christian faces.

> Finally, be strong in the Lord and in his mighty
> power. (Ephesians 6:10)

He is talking about the daily confrontation we have in the battles against sin and the tempter. But what does it mean to "be strong in the Lord and in his mighty power"? The word "strong" could be exchanged by "fill yourself with power" in the Lord, for it is the translation of a Greek word whose root is *dunamis,* "power." This power that Paul is talking about is the power that comes through the Holy Spirit. In Acts 1:8, Jesus said,

> But you will receive power when the Holy Spirit
> comes on you; and you will be my witnesses in
> Jerusalem, and in all Judea and Samaria, and to the
> ends of the earth. (Acts 1:8)

Power is crucial to overcoming spiritual struggles, emotional anguish, temptations of the flesh, diabolical provocations, and the appeals of the world. If we try to overcome these challenges by our human strength, we will lose. The power is poured out on us by the Holy Spirit, so we need to fill ourselves with the Spirit daily so that we will not fall into the traps of Satan and his demons. That is why Paul also wrote,

> So I say, walk by the Spirit, and you will not gratify
> the desires of the flesh. (Galatians 5:16)

The secret of not walking in the flesh is to be filled with the Spirit. But how can we be filled with the power of the Holy Spirit? Paul answers this question by writing to the Ephesians,

> Do not get drunk on wine, which leads to debauchery. Instead, be filled with the Spirit, speaking to one another with psalms, hymns, and songs from the Spirit. Sing and make music from your heart to the Lord, always giving thanks to God the Father for everything, in the name of our Lord Jesus Christ. Submit to one another out of reverence for Christ. (Ephesians 5:18–21)

In other words, he guides you to abstain from things that, like wine, intoxicate your mind, leading you to sinful attitudes. Maybe for you it's some kind of drink, or maybe entertainment, or even some sensual pleasure.

With what have you filled your heart in order to quiet your anxieties? Just as alcoholic drinks inebriate the sorrows, what have you been drinking to anesthetize your soul? Paul says not to get drunk anymore with these things but to learn how to fill yourself with the Spirit!

Paul is teaching us two simple steps: empty yourself of everything that makes you sin and distracts you, and fill yourself with everything that relates to the Lord, in worship, praise, and prayers.

In the last chapter, you were invited to do this in your closed room. Cry before the Lord, confess your sins, worship genuinely, and meditate on his word. Now you need to turn this into a lifestyle! Learn to take time every day to be filled with the presence of the Holy Spirit!

If we live the way Paul talks, we will have a life filled with the Spirit. This is the reason why in Ephesians 6:10 Paul does not say to be strengthened "by" the Lord, but "in" the Lord. The change may be small grammatically, but in our relationship with God, from the moment we surrender our life to Jesus, it must be immersed in him!

Just as in baptism the person is immersed in the water, representing his immersion in Jesus Christ and his Spirit, now we must live immersed in his presence! We must immerse our homes, our dreams, our minds, our bodies, our agendas, and our activities in Christ! We cannot use Jesus as an occasional source of power and spiritual satisfaction. We must immerse ourselves in him, live in Christ, and walk in the Spirit!

The Heavenly Father doesn't want to be a genie in the lamp causing you to come to him only when you have needs. He wants to be your Father, to walk with you every day. He is interested in every beat of your heart.

The first step in emptying ourselves, so we can be filled by the Spirit, can be helped through the biblical practice of fasting! Fasting is a spiritual discipline practiced by men and women of God. In the Old Testament, the prophets fasted. Jesus fasted, the apostles fasted, the early Christians fasted, and we must learn to fast! Unfortunately, this important practice has been abandoned by people who teach that fasting is no longer necessary for the Christian.

Jesus fasted at the beginning of his ministry (Matthew 4:2; Mark 1:13; Luke 4:1–2). This alone should be enough to convince us that fasting should be practiced by Jesus's disciples. Christ taught that fasting should not be done in a hypocritical way, teaching how it should be done (Matthew 6:16–18), making it clear that his disciples would fast. This teaching was so clear that the church in the book of Acts continued to practice fasting as Jesus taught.

Fasting is to the body what prayer is to the soul. It is meaningless if it is not genuinely a cry for divine intervention. Fasting is one way how we get our entire lives to plead, cry out, and ask the only one who can answer! Jesus clearly taught the importance of insistence in prayer.

> So I say to you: Ask and it will be given to you; seek
> and you will find; knock and the door will be opened
> to you. For everyone who asks receives; the one who
> seeks finds; and to the one who knocks, the door will

be opened. Which of you fathers, if your son asks for a fish, will give him a snake instead? Or if he asks for an egg, will give him a scorpion? If you then, though you are evil, know how to give good gifts to your children, how much more will your Father in heaven give the Holy Spirit to those who ask him! (Luke 11:9–13)

Luke makes it clear that Peter was without food when he literally went into ecstasy *(ekstasis)* when he had the divine vision of the sheet coming down from heaven (Acts 10:10). Although this fast doesn't seem to have been voluntary, and it probably wasn't long, Luke gives this information because it was relevant to him.

The church at Antioch also fasted (Acts 13:2). Luke makes it clear that the fast was part of seeking the voice of God when the Holy Spirit spoke to separate Paul and Barnabas for a mission. Luke also informs us that Paul and Barnabas fasted and prayed to choose elders for the churches in Lystra, Iconium, and Antioch (Acts 14:23), showing that fasting was a practice taught in the churches they planted.

Fasting helps us to quiet the voice of our flesh and to turn completely to the Lord. It is not just staying without food but involves dedicating oneself to praying intensely and meditating on the Word of God. In fasting, we open our hearts to hear God more clearly, coming closer to him! In fasting we sadden our souls; we humble ourselves in seeking the intervention of the Heavenly Father.

Jesus said that there are types of demons that come out only with much fasting and prayer (Matthew 17:21). There are spiritual battles that will need your fasting. When we deal with deep involvements in sorcery, for example, we may need to fast in order to be completely free. Intense practices of sin, such as addictions and other compulsions, must be overcome through fasting and prayer! If you are still dealing with repetitive sins, fast and pray! But beware. Do not fast like the Pharisees, who let people see that they were fasting to be considered as holy men (Matthew 6:16–18). No one needs to know that you are fasting, only God!

How about today you empty yourself and start filling with the Spirit? Take time out of your daily schedule to read the Bible, pray, and praise God in your private place. Choose to pour out your heart before Jesus, and he will pour out his Spirit on you! Maybe you need to spend some time fasting! Strengthen yourself in the Lord! Learn to read the Bible and meditate on it daily. It is the spiritual food that invigorates our souls, strengthens our hearts, and gives us wisdom. Dedicate time every day to be with the Lord, and see how he will strengthen you!

Day 27

WEARING THE ARMOR OF GOD

When the apostle Paul wrote his letter to Ephesus, he was in prison for preaching the Gospel. He constantly saw soldiers coming in and out, wearing their polished armor. These suits of armor were distinguished from each other by the rank of the soldier. The higher the rank, the more beautiful the armor. It's in this context that Paul wrote,

> Put on the full armor of God, so that you can take your stand against the devil's schemes. (Ephesians 6:11)

The Greek word used by Paul here referring to armor is not the common armor of an ordinary soldier but the armor of an officer! This armor had the emperor's symbol engraved on it. Wearing this armor represented the emperor himself. It was the symbol of imperial authority. To stand up before a person wearing armor like this was the same as standing before the emperor himself! Paul guides us to put on God's armor to face Satan. Our armor carries the insignia of our King on our chest, so demons, powers, and principalities tremble before our authority. Look what Paul said about God's insignia in us.

> And you also were included in Christ when you heard the message of truth, the gospel of your salvation. When you believed, you were marked in him with a seal, the promised Holy Spirit (Ephesians 1:13)

When we understand that on our chest is engraved the Holy Spirit, and that our enemies will see this mark from afar, we start realizing the responsibility that it means to be a Christian. We carry the name of Christ in our own names, identifying ourselves as "Christians." We must, therefore, honor this mark and the King's name by living an honorable life according to God's righteousness. Jesus's name and his Holy Spirit within us give us authority.

> He replied, "I saw Satan fall like lightning from heaven. I have given you authority to trample on snakes and scorpions and to overcome all the power of the enemy; nothing will harm you." (Luke 10:18–19)

God's mark involves responsibility and authority! When we consciously wear God's armor, we know that we are officers of the King. The apostle lists the items in this armor; however, we need to understand that these are not mystical descriptions, where we simply take note of the items being put on us. No, the items are very powerful weapons of defense and attack, but they need to be truly assimilated into our lives as a royal garment that protects us from evil attacks! The items are spiritual weapons we need to wear every day!

Paul says that the armor serves to keep us firm! This is one of the most repeated words in this chapter and in other texts dealing with the spiritual battle against Satan.

> Submit yourselves, then, to God. <u>Resist</u> the devil, and he will flee from you. (James 4:7)

> Be alert and of sober mind. Your enemy the devil prowls around like a roaring lion looking for someone to devour. <u>Resist</u> him, standing firm in the faith, because you know that the family of believers throughout the world is undergoing the same kind of sufferings. (1 Peter 5:8–9)

Resisting the devil is our main task in the spiritual battle. He tempts us, set traps to make us fall into sin, tries to throw us against each other, and casts in our minds doubts, discouragement, and sadness while trying to make us believe in lies! Paul, James, and Peter are saying the same thing: resist the devil!

Unfortunately, many Christians have faced Satan without any armor. They face evil with their own human strength. They believe in their wisdom and capacities, so they suffer great oppression from the devil, falling many times. We will always lose if we fight Satan with our own strength. We need God's armor for the battles we face daily. Unfortunately, many Christians are being beaten because of their ignorance. Don't underestimate Satan!

There are Christians losing the battle against the devil through activism, stress, and depression. People are captured again by the chains of pornography and other sexual addictions. Some Christians allow themselves to be immobilized again by demonic addictions. There are believers enslaved by the debts that Satan led them to incur when they fell into the sin of greed, spending their energy and health to acquire superfluous things to maintain an expensive and wasteful lifestyle! The same Satan who takes advantage of greed uses loan sharks to keep people imprisoned by money. There are also Christians who are hurt, wounded in their souls, and bound by the emotional injuries of the devil who always reopens the wounds so they never heal. These people go to church but do not allow Jesus to enter and change everything in their hearts. They are Christians. They are saved by the grace of Christ. But because they do not wear God's armor that gives authority, they walk according to the flesh and live a defeated life!

The need to use armor means we are at war. So you need to wear it and declare war against Satan in your life, in your mind, your body, and in your family! Decide to oppose him in all areas. Take risks to honor your king! Fight the good fight; resist Satan with all your strength. Make the decision to win back every inch that in the past you gave to the devil. Pray, cry, repent, and cling to Christ with all your strength, but don't take another step backward. Decide to fight until the end!

I remember one day arriving at my church after arguing with my wife. Do you know those silly fights between husband and wife? When I arrived at the church, a sister came to me saying that there was a demonic woman in need of deliverance. At that moment, I thought, *How will I cast out this demon if I sinned, fighting with my wife today?* I tried to call my wife, but she wouldn't answer. I went to a room and prayed, confessing my sins. I cried for the foolish mistake I had made, asking God for forgiveness. At that moment, I asked the Lord, "How can I cast out the demons of this woman today, Lord?" Then the Lord reminded me that the authority I needed was his, not mine! It was him I needed to trust, not me! My sins were forgiven, and what I needed to do was just put on the armor of God. Then I went to the demon-possessed woman and cast out the demons. They resisted, but in the end, they left. Later, I managed to talk to my wife and asked her for forgiveness, and then we were well again. We never know when Satan confronts us, so we must always be vigilant!

The apostle Paul said we need to wear the belt of truth, the breastplate of righteousness, the sandals of Gospel preaching, the shield of faith, the helmet of salvation, and the sword of the Spirit! Wearing the belt of truth means that our life needs to be involved in truth. There is no place for Satan's deception or his demonic doctrines. There is no place for lying! If you are in the habit of lying, even if it's enhancing a story, you need to confess and get rid of this demonic practice! If you usually lie so as not to hurt people, remember that the devil is the father of lies (John 8:44)! In some countries, lying is a very serious problem. With the intention of protecting someone's honor, lying becomes a common practice. When a culture is based on lies, everything that is called honorable is actually an illusion!

The breastplate of righteousness means that our chest, where the heart is, needs to be dressed in God's righteousness. Justice means God's will. Does your heart seek to do God's will or your own? Are your attitudes righteous or unfair? In the Bible, God's justice is manifested when we feed the poor, take care of people suffering, like widows and orphans, show mercy to our offenders, and are hospitable to foreigners. God's justice is expressed not only in relation to what he doesn't want us to do but especially in relation to what he wants us to accomplish! Have you been an agent of God's justice in the lives of people around you?

> Religion that God our Father accepts as pure and faultless is this: to look after orphans and widows in their distress and to keep oneself from being polluted by the world. (James 1:27)

The feet fitted with the readiness that comes with the gospel of peace (Ephesians 6:15) means that we must always be ready to walk toward the lost, those who suffer and lack God's glory. This means we need to be proclaimers of the good news of Christ, the gospel of peace. We are not soldiers of a kingdom that just protects itself from an invader. In fact, we are the invaders going to the kingdom of darkness to pluck out of hell those who are trapped. We must be ready to walk toward the lost and proclaim the gospel of Christ! When we truly understand that we are the light of the world, we no longer fear the darkness. In fact, we learn to walk toward it fearlessly! When we invade the darkness, we realize the value of our light, we discover the meaning of our life, and we are amazed at the depth of God's grace and power!

The shield of faith is our main weapon of defense (Ephesians 6:16). We need to learn to move our shield toward the fiery darts sent by our enemy. Often the darts thrown by demons are words of discouragement, terrible offenses, or significant events that try to bring us down. Satan attacks us using people close to us, from our work, our family, where he tries to hit us with a poisoned dart. But when we learn to fight using our faith, we move our shield in the direction of these attacks. We immediately reject the discouraging and poisoned words, not believing in what people say about us but only what the Bible says. We reject the doubts, the seed of incredulity, the false beliefs, and every type of attack through our shield of faith!

The helmet of salvation is also indispensable (Ephesians 6:17). We must not enter battle with Satan without the certainty of our salvation. If you have not yet truly given your life to Jesus, do not wait. Do it now! Jesus saves us and gives us the certainty of his salvation. It is by faith that you trust in Jesus's salvation and appropriate what he did at the cross for you. In Christ we are rescued, forgiven, adopted to be God's children, and sealed by his Spirit, and nothing and no one can take away this certainty from us! Read what the apostle Paul wrote.

> In all these things we are more than conquerors through him who loved us. For I am convinced that neither death nor life, neither angels nor demons, neither the present nor the future, nor any powers, neither height nor depth, nor anything else in all creation, will be able to separate us from the love of God that is in Christ Jesus our Lord. (Romans 8:37–39)

Finally, Paul speaks about the sword of the Spirit (Ephesians 6:17). The sword is the Word of God. It is with this sword that Jesus refuted Satan's tempting arguments in the desert (Matthew 4:1–11). With the Word of God, we can overcome the devil every day! We must learn to meditate on it day and night. Feed our souls with this spiritual bread! When the Word of God is in your heart, in your mind, on your lips, and in your attitudes, fighting Satan becomes very easy!

Which items of this armor are you already using? Which ones still need to be put on? You can pray to God asking him to dress you with each one of these items. Pray in humility hoping that God will speak to you. Pray and wait in silence. He will talk and show you what you need to do!

Day 28

WHO IS OUR ENEMY?

I n Ephesians 6, the apostle Paul also tells us about our enemy.

> For our struggle is not against flesh and blood, but
> against the rulers, against the authorities, against the
> powers of this dark world and against the spiritual
> forces of evil in the heavenly realms. (Ephesians 6:12)

Before saying who our enemy is, Paul emphasized who he is not!
Our fight is not against people, although it often seems to be. We
suffer persecution, opposition, and temptation because people offend
us, deceive us, tell lies, manipulate us, or even physically attack us.

It is natural to think that they are our enemies when in fact our
true enemy is a spiritual being who falsely engenders attacks using
people. We need to understand that our enemy is not our oppressive
husband or wife, our aggressive neighbor, the unfair boss, the woman
who tries to seduce another's husband, or even the criminal who lures
victims in society. Our enemy is not the Hindu priest, the Buddhist
monk, the hating imam, or anyone who, due to sin and spiritual
blindness, offends or attacks us. Our adversaries are not these even
if they are used by the devil to attack us. It is very important to
recognize this so we can focus on our true enemy!

The apostle Paul lists a series of words that help us to know
our true enemy. He begins by saying that our struggle is against
the "powers." In Greek, he used the word *arches*, which means

"first ones" or "rulers" and can also be translated as "princes" or "principalities." These princes are the ones who hold the power over many people. They are the demonic rulers who systematically direct the implantation of Satan's evil reign on earth.

In the book of Daniel, in chapter 10, the prophet describes a tremendous experience he had with God. After twenty-one days of prayer and fasting, he had an encounter with an angel of the Lord. This angel said that God had heard his prayer from the first day he was praying, but this angel was opposed by the "Prince of Persia," a demonic prince ruling over the nation of Persia. The angel said that he called the archangel Michael, the "Prince of the nation of Israel," to help him in this fight. Consequently, he got the victory and thus was able to give the answer to the prophet's prayers!

What a stupendous vision of what happens when we are in a spiritual battle. The prophet Daniel understood why his prayers seemed to be not answered, giving us also a deep understanding of what occurs in the spiritual world when we pray and fast. Satan tries to keep our prayers from being answered, but if we persevere, he cannot win.

I believe Paul is referring to these demonic princes too! Our adversary has power over people and nations. He exercises authority over cultures, society, and many pagan philosophies. Now let's think about your own culture for a moment! Which spiritual principalities were responsible for shaping the values of your society? Why are some countries so affected by violence and death? Revenge and unforgiveness destroy many families in such countries. Why are some cultures that worship gods of destruction surrounded by destruction and poverty? Who taught the caste system and the doctrine of reincarnation in Hinduism? Which demonic principalities taught Buddhist rituals with the false promise of spiritual elevation? In fact, my intention with these questions is to make you understand that every pagan religion is ruled and organized by a hierarchy of demons and not simply by people.

In the prophet Daniel's time, he was under the oppressive influence of Babylon, pressured to follow that demonic culture and enjoy the same wicked pleasures that everyone was enjoying. However, the prophet resisted with all his strength, submitting himself only to the Lord (Daniel 1:8–17). He decided not to surrender to the sensual and idolatrous appeals of his time. Today we also suffer the oppression of these demonic principalities influencing our society. The sphere of action of these principalities manifests in politics, economy, culture, fashion, and art, influencing us through our neighbors, family, television, and music in ways that we are hardly aware of.

Our fight is against these principalities. We are pressured by them to embrace a sex life without limits and without commitments, to seek enrichment at all costs, and to defend ideologies that lead us to a blind and oppressive nationalism. They pressure us to manipulate people to achieve our goals, to dress as they dress, to speak as they speak, making us their puppets. We must resist and fight against these forces, abstaining from everything that is under their power by praying all the time.

The fact that the prophet Daniel prayed for twenty-one days is also important. It could have been twenty-two or ten days. What matters is that he decided to pray until receiving God's answer. When we pray, we must do it with faith, believing that God will answer.

> Very truly I tell you, whoever believes in me will do the works I have been doing, and they will do even greater things than these, because I am going to the Father. And I will do whatever you ask in my name, so that the Father may be glorified in the Son. You may ask me for anything in my name, and I will do it. (John 14:12–14)

> Because anyone who comes to him must believe that he exists and that he rewards those who earnestly seek him. (Hebrews 11:6)

> If any of you lacks wisdom, you should ask God, who gives generously to all without finding fault, and it

will be given to you. But when you ask, you must believe and not doubt, because the one who doubts is like a wave of the sea, blown and tossed by the wind. That person should not expect to receive anything from the Lord. Such a person is double-minded and unstable in all they do. (James 1:5–8)

Daniel knew that God would answer so he did not give up until his answer came. He was not aware that a spiritual battle was going on while he prayed, but he persisted until the answer came! Have you prayed until you received God's answer? The answer can be positive or negative. The word can be healing when we pray for an illness, but it can also be a no like the one given to Paul when he prayed for the thorn in his flesh to be taken away (2 Corinthians 12:7). God had a greater purpose in Paul's life than to heal him. But Paul was at peace because he received his answer! God told him, "My grace is sufficient for you, for my power is made perfect in weakness" (2 Corinthians 12:9).

Like Daniel, when we pray for something and the answer doesn't come immediately, we must be aware that maybe a spiritual battle is going on that we are not aware of. If we stop praying, the battle will be lost and the answer will never come! But if we pray persistently, believing that God's answer will come, we will experience great things from the Lord! Look what Jesus said about perseverance in prayer.

So I say to you: Ask and it will be given to you; seek and you will find; knock and the door will be opened to you. For everyone who asks receives; the one who seeks finds; and to the one who knocks, the door will be opened. (Luke 11:9–10)

If we could see what happens in the spiritual world and how powerful our prayers are, we would invest much more time praying.

We also would resist the principalities in this world in constant prayer, like the prophet Daniel.

I once preached in a remote Hindu village in India. There were people who had never heard the gospel before, and I could present Jesus in a very simple way! I spoke of Jesus's miracles and presented him as the true God who came to this world to save us. In the end, I appealed to those who desired to abandon the false gods and give their lives to Jesus. Some came to the front, and among them, a young man said, "You told that Jesus healed many people and that he has power over all things, and that he is here today. Well, I brought my sick mother so Jesus can heal her. She had a stroke! She is sitting at the back!" I looked at the back of that place and there was a lady with a paralyzed hand.

I confess that my faith was very small. After praying for the people in the front, I went to pray for the lady. When I started praying for her, the lady started screaming in pain. I stopped and asked what was happening. She said her arm was burning. The paralyzed arm was burning, and I was not touching her! At that moment, I understood that God wanted to heal her! I prayed again, asking for her healing, and the woman screamed as if her arm were undergoing surgery right there. I prayed for forty minutes with that woman until she stopped screaming. I opened my eyes and saw her hand perfectly healed while she moved her fingers before her face. She was happy that Jesus had healed her so powerfully, and I was amazed to see it before my eyes.

I don't know why I had to pray for forty minutes. Jesus could have answered in one minute! But he did not, so I kept praying until he answered. Maybe there was a spiritual battle going on that I was not aware of. The fact is after persevering in prayer, the answer came! Not always the answer to what we ask God for is what we want. But that day it was! She was healed!

Day 29

CLOSING THE GAPS

We are at war, and we can't ignore this. While we are in this world, living in this flesh that suffers the consequences of our sins and of others, we must be alert not to fall into the devil's trap. Our adversary is cunning, manipulative, and a liar. Paul described him as a prince, as we saw yesterday. But he also called him "authorities" (Ephesians 6:12). But what does that mean?

The word "authorities" means they had authorization. In Ephesians 6:12, the apostle Paul refers to these authorities as personal beings who have the authority or rights over people. But do Satan and his demons have authority or authorization? Unfortunately, yes. After Adam and Eve ate of the fruit in the Garden of Eden, the devil became the "Prince of this world" possessing rights over people through sin! Read what Paul also says.

> In your anger do not sin: Do not let the sun go down
> while you are still angry, and do not give the devil a
> foothold. (Ephesians 4:26–27)

To give the devil a foothold is to give him permission over something in your life. When we surrender to anger, the text assures us we are giving an opportunity to the devil! Satan has authority and a right over people who have given themselves to a life of sin. The apostle John also talks about this when he wrote the following:

> The one who does what is sinful is of the devil, because the devil has been sinning from the beginning. The reason the Son of God appeared was to destroy the devil's work. No one who is born of God will continue to sin, because God's seed remains in them; they cannot go on sinning, because they have been born of God. (1 John 3:8–9)

This does not mean that everyone who sins belongs to the devil because we are all sinners (Romans 3:23). However, those who remain in sin belong to him! The true Christian possesses in himself the "seed of God," as John said, and with this, he cannot live in sin. Therefore, he is constrained by the Holy Spirit to get rid of sin, repent, and confess to God. However, if he does not repent or turn away from sin but does the opposite, embracing more and more the sinful life, evidently he does not possess the "seed of God" in his life, which is the Holy Spirit. He is mistaken, for he belongs to the devil!

Read what the apostle Paul is teaching to Timothy about how he should minister to those who resist the gospel.

> And the Lord's servant must not be quarrelsome but must be kind to everyone, able to teach, not resentful. Opponents must be gently instructed, in the hope that God will grant them repentance leading them to a knowledge of the truth, and that they will come to their senses and escape from the trap of the devil, who has taken them captive to do his will. (2 Timothy 2:24–26)

Timothy was taught to instruct gently, hoping that God would bring repentance and the knowledge of the truth. Then they are set free from the trap of the devil. Everyone who is not saved in Jesus is captive to the will of Satan and his demons! Therefore, these demons are called authorities, because they received authorization through sin to keep people captive. It is through sin that they have authorization!

Have you ever noticed how the religions around you distort the concept of sin? In fact, what they do is deny its existence. Demons know that if people think they are not sinners—that is, that they don't need to repent and confess their sins—they will automatically give the devil authority over their lives.

Authorities are the demons who have a right over the lives of people who gave themselves over to a life of sin. Take, for example, the life of Saul, a king who was blessed by God. However, Saul chose to disobey the Lord several times and sinned against him. After letting himself be carried away by fear (1 Samuel 13:5–7), King Saul succumbed to the pressure of the crowd and broke a very serious commandment (1 Samuel 13:8–10). Saul did not care about pleasing God but about pleasing the people. When the prophet Samuel arrived where the king was, he declared to him that his disobedience would have great consequences. Later, after being strictly guided by God not to take any spoil of war against the Amalekite people because he should have destroyed everything, he disobeyed again (1 Samuel 15). Consequently, the Lord withdrew his blessing on his life. What happened next is that an evil spirit came upon Saul, and from that moment on, he was tormented by him (1 Samuel 6:14). This spirit had authorization over Saul because of his disobedience!

Paul also calls our enemies "powers of this dark world" (Ephesians 6:12). This term comes from the Greek word *kosmokratoras*, which literally means "Those who hold the world."

These powers are nothing more than demonic forces that control, dominate, manipulate, and imprison people. If they have authority over something, then they manipulate it!

If you are enslaved by a hidden sin from which you cannot free yourself, there is a high probability that you are under the dominion of these evil dominators. They are the ones who promote addiction, imprisoning the mind through sin and making the heart obstinate. I met many people imprisoned by these spirits, many without even realizing they were under their control. These demons manipulate people so people say whatever they want, hurt those they want to hurt, and oppress those they want to oppress. These people become channels for the demons to exert power over others.

To overcome these powers, we must confess and renounce our sins. We need to bring to light what is hidden in our hearts. Satan will always have power over hidden sins! Although if we want to be free from the dominion that sin exerts on us, whether through vices or "pet" sins, then we need to confess them to a brother or sister in Christ! See what James says about this.

> Therefore confess your sins to each other and pray for each other so that you may be healed. The prayer of a righteous person is powerful and effective. (James 5:16)

The forgiveness of our sins comes from repentance and confession to God, but the healing and deliverance from the power of sin come from our confession to a brother or sister. Confessing a sin to someone requires courage, and it is an act of humiliation. Admitting to a brother involves admitting weakness, exposing the darkness hidden in your heart, and allowing the light of Christ to reach you!

When I ask new believers to confess their sins to a brother or sister in Christ, they usually resist. Nobody wants their infamous stories to be known. We are professionals at hiding dirt under the carpet of our hearts. We are full of rotten things stored away, and we are ashamed to even think of the possibility of someone discovering what has happened. Thus, by not confessing to others, these sins continue to exercise power over us. We continue to fall back into the same sins and keep giving power to Satan.

Today can be a very special day. How about making a radical decision to break every authority and dominion that Satan may have over you? Take a paper and write on it all your recurring sins. Don't justify them; just write them down! Also, describe what kind of sinful thoughts you usually have. Ask God for a brother or sister in Christ who can hear you and pray for you. This can be a leader in your church, your pastor, or any other mature brother or sister. Sit with this person in a safe and quiet environment and read everything you wrote in a spirit of prayer, confessing before him or her and God. Ask for this brother or sister to pray for you! If you do this with sincere repentance, you will surely experience the deliverance that only God gives. If there is any demonic authority over your life, it will be broken!

Day 30

BACK HOME!

This is the last chapter of our devotional. If you have still struggled with sins, still feel wounded in your heart, perhaps still oppressed by Satan in your life, I advise you to go back and reread the previous days. But do this by meditating carefully on God's Word. Meditate and choose to obey! Listening to God's voice and not obeying him is the same as rejecting God.

Maybe you say you don't have the strength to overcome the evil inside you. And I affirm that you are right! Nobody has enough strength to overcome sin, bitterness, and rejection, much less Satan himself in your life. If we do not seek this strength in Jesus, we will never succeed. For Jesus has all the strength, authority, and power we need! Our role is to do our part trusting completely in Christ and his power!

Jesus calls you to be his disciple. The journey has just begun. But there is still much you need to learn! When we put Jesus at the center of our lives, repent, and renounce everything that opposes him, we enter the kingdom of God. We return to the Father's house! This was Jesus's message inviting people to his kingdom.

> From that time on Jesus began to preach, Repent, for
> the kingdom of heaven has come near. (Matthew 4:17)

By "near," Jesus means that the kingdom is at your disposal, is "at hand." The kingdom of God is within your reach! Just repent and believe! If you have repented of your sins genuinely, renounced the evil practices of your life, and rejected Satan and all his influence, putting your faith completely in Jesus Christ, then you are saved! Jesus has truly set you free! You have entered the kingdom of God and now Jesus is your king! The moment we believe, we are made a new creature.

> Therefore, if anyone is in Christ, the new creation has come: The old has gone, the new is here! (2 Corinthians 5:17)

The apostle Paul also speaks of this new life we have in Christ and the role that the Holy Spirit plays in us.

> Therefore, there is now no condemnation for those who are in Christ Jesus, because through Christ Jesus the law of the Spirit who gives life has set you free from the law of sin and death. For what the law was powerless to do because it was weakened by the flesh, God did by sending his own Son in the likeness of sinful flesh to be a sin offering. And so he condemned sin in the flesh, in order that the righteous requirement of the law might be fully met in us, who do not live according to the flesh but according to the Spirit. Those who live according to the flesh have their minds set on what the flesh desires; but those who live in accordance with the Spirit have their minds set on what the Spirit desires. The mind governed by the flesh is death, but the mind governed by the Spirit is life and peace. The mind governed by the flesh is hostile to God; it does not submit to God's law, nor can it do so. Those who are in the realm of the flesh cannot please God. (Romans 8:1–8)

If you are saved, you are a new creature and the Holy Spirit lives in you! It is up to you now to fill yourself with his presence every day. You must learn to hear and obey the voice of the Spirit so that you may walk following his guidance and not your flesh. As you fill yourself with the Spirit, he will bring forth in you the fruit of the Spirit and give you gifts. Learn to pray that the Father will bear this fruit in you daily in your actions and thoughts.

> But the fruit of the Spirit is love, joy, peace, forbearance, kindness, goodness, faithfulness, gentleness and self-control. Against such things there is no law. (Galatians 5:22–23)

The only way we can overcome sin is by submitting ourselves to Christ and his Spirit every day. If we walk in the spirit, we will overcome our fleshly desires, as discussed before. But if we try to overcome sin with our own strength, we will lose!

For this, our faith in Christ needs to be based on three times: yesterday, today, and tomorrow! Yesterday means that we need to learn everything that God already did in the past in the lives of his servants. Therefore, read the Bible! Learn from the lives of David, Jeremiah, Jesus, and Paul. Read every day, and meditate on the spiritual treasures of God! Study it in depth!

However, our faith in Christ must also be for today. Jesus did not only act in the past. He continues to act today!

> Remember your leaders, who spoke the word of God to you. Consider the outcome of their way of life and imitate their faith. Jesus Christ is the same yesterday and today and forever. (Hebrews 13:7–8)

We must imitate the faith of these great men today. Do as they did; believe as they believed! If we only know what Jesus did but do not do the same, then we are hypocrites. Look what Jesus and Paul said about this.

> Very truly I tell you, whoever believes in me will do the works I have been doing, and they will do even greater things than these, because I am going to the Father. (John 14:12)

> Follow my example, as I follow the example of Christ. (1 Corinthians 11:1)

We need to act today in faith, imitating Abraham, who believed that God could resurrect his son. We need to act with courage, as David faced Goliath, believing that God was with him. We need to trust in God's provision today, as Moses led the whole nation of Israel to the desert believing that God would sustain them miraculously. The Bible is not a book for you to enjoy as entertainment. It is for you to learn from, be inspired by, hear God's voice through, and follow the examples of these men and women of God! Make the Bible stories once again alive in your life today!

But our faith also needs to be firm in Jesus for tomorrow! It must look to the future! One day Jesus Christ will return and take his church to live with him. If you die before this day, you will enjoy his presence in paradise. In heaven, we will have a glorified body that no longer suffers, for there is no sin or evil. There we will be able to eat from the tree of life! In other words, we will return to God's paradise where we will live with him eternally. Read what the Bible says about this.

> Then will appear the sign of the Son of Man in heaven. And then all the peoples of the earth will mourn when they see the Son of Man coming on the clouds of heaven, with power and great glory. And he will send his angels with a loud trumpet call, and they will gather his elect from the four winds, from one end of the heavens to the other. (Matthew 24:30–31)

But our citizenship is in heaven. And we eagerly await a Savior from there, the Lord Jesus Christ, who, by the power that enables him to bring everything under his control, will transform our lowly bodies so that they will be like his glorious body. (Philippians 3:20–21)

When Christ, who is your life, appears, then you also will appear with him in glory. (Colossians 3:4)

Whoever has ears, let them hear what the Spirit says to the churches. To the one who is victorious, I will give the right to eat from the tree of life, which is in the paradise of God. (Revelation 2:7)

Then the angel showed me the river of the water of life, as clear as crystal, flowing from the throne of God and of the Lamb down the middle of the great street of the city. On each side of the river stood the tree of life, bearing twelve crops of fruit, yielding its fruit every month. And the leaves of the tree are for the healing of the nations. No longer will there be any curse. The throne of God and of the Lamb will be in the city, and his servants will serve him. They will see his face, and his name will be on their foreheads. There will be no more night. They will not need the light of a lamp or the light of the sun, for the Lord God will give them light. And they will reign for ever and ever. (Revelation 22:1–5)

Jesus will return, and then we will reign with him! But there is still much to do. We must not cross our arms and wait passively for Christ's return. We must wait, but actively. We have been set free by Christ and now can also set others free. The world still lies under the evil one (1 John 5:19), and we need to break the chains that still hold the people around us.

Just as Peter, James, John, and the other disciples were saved by Jesus Christ and then sent into the world to free and save the lost, you and I are also sent. We have in our hands the gospel of peace, the power of God, and his command to go! He gave us authority and expects us to obey him.

> He said to them: Go throughout the whole world and preach the gospel to all people. Whoever believes and is baptized will be saved; whoever does not believe will be condemned. Believers will be given the power to perform miracles: they will drive out demons in my name; they will speak in strange tongues; if they pick up snakes or drink any poison, they will not be harmed; they will place their arms on sick people, and these will get well. (Mark 16:15–18)

I believe this. What about you? May God bless you and use you powerfully for the praise of his glory!

Printed in the United States
by Baker & Taylor Publisher Services